BREATH of GOD

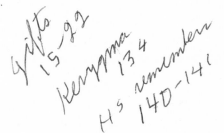

"Rev. Dave Pivonka's reflections on the Holy Spirit are refreshing. One cannot say enough about the third person of the Blessed Trinity, who is the Mystery of the Mystery. This Mystery is a person who encounters us in the grace of the moment."

Most Rev. Sam Jacobs
Bishop Emeritus of the Diocese of Houma-Thibodaux

"If you want your life to become a new adventure, read this book."

Chris Stefanick
Founder and president of Real Life Catholic

"I have witnessed Fr. Dave living under the action and inspiration of the Holy Spirit for more than twenty years. I can't think of a better guide to introduce you to the person and power of the Holy Spirit."

Mark Berchem
Founder and president of NET Ministries

"In *Breath of God*, Rev. Dave Pivonka invites us to open our lives more fully to the Holy Spirit. He promises us the adventure of a lifetime—led by the Spirit in wonderful, unexpected ways, guided to right choices, empowered to endure trials, healed of emotional turmoil, gifted for daily life and service, and much more. In each chapter, Fr. Dave shows us how to encounter the Spirit, come to know him better, and put his graces into action. *Breath of God* will bring you an exciting and joyful experience of the Holy Spirit—I urge you to read it."

Bert Ghezzi
Author of *The Heart of Catholicism*

DAVE PIVONKA, T.O.R.

BREATH of GOD

Living a Life Led by the Holy Spirit

Gifts of H.S. by Pope Franca   Pg 15-23

AVE MARIA PRESS AVE Notre Dame, Indiana

Founded in 1865, Ave Maria Press is a ministry of the United States Province of Holy Cross.

www.avemariapress.com

Paperback: ISBN-13 978-1-59471-580-8

E-book: ISBN-13 978-1-59471-581-5

Cover image "Holy Spirit, Bring Your Fire" © Ren, renwowart.com.

Cover and text design by Andy Wagoner.

Printed and bound in the United States of America.

Library of Congress Cataloging-in-Publication Data
Pivonka, Dave.
  Breath of God : living a life led by the Holy Spirit / Dave Pivonka, T.O.R.
     pages cm
  Includes bibliographical references.
  ISBN 978-1-59471-580-8 -- ISBN 1-59471-580-7
  1. Holy Spirit. 2. Christian life--Catholic authors. I. Title.
  BT121.3.P58 2015
  231'.3--dc23
                                        2015018844

TO THE SPIRIT of JESUS

WHO HAS GIVEN ME LIFE.
COME HOLY SPIRIT.

If the Spirit of the one who raised Jesus from the dead dwells in you, the one who raised Christ from the dead will give life to your mortal bodies also, through his Spirit that dwells in you.

—Romans 8:11

CONTENTS

INTRODUCTION

> The Spirit and the bride say, "Come." Let the hearer say, "Come." Let the one who thirsts come forward, and the one who wants it receive the gift of life-giving water.
>
> —Revelation 22:17

"Dad, why is there a dog up there over the tabernacle?"

My dad turned to me with a puzzled look on his face and asked what I meant.

Pointing up above the altar and tabernacle I said, "There, up there. Why is there a painting of a dog there?" My dad looked to where I was pointing and still was confused. "David, I don't see what you mean." I took Dad by the arm and we walked closer to the altar. "Right there!" I then pointed out the dog's ears and snout. It looked like a Dachshund, but I wasn't positive. A big grin came over Dad's face, and he chuckled. "David, that's not a dog; it's a dove, the Holy Spirit. Those aren't ears; they are wings, and that is the dove's beak and head, not the nose of a dog. But I can see how it does kind of look like a dog."

And so began my relationship with the Holy Spirit. I was probably six or seven at the time and was confused as to why the Holy Spirit would look so much like a dog. I would later learn that there are many symbols for the Holy Spirit beyond a dog and dove. There is also fire, wind, water, wine, rays of light, clouds, and oil, and they all represent the Holy Spirit in some way.

However, thanks to a dear friend of mine, I have recently discovered a new image that I love. The Celts had a name for the Holy Spirit, *An Geadh-Glas*, translated as "the Wild Goose." Not a fragile, domesticated dove but a wild, untamed goose. Immediately when my friend told me about the Wild Goose, it resonated in my heart. I thought to myself, "Yes, that's perfect."

Several times a week I go for a walk in my neighborhood, often through a large, old cemetery. In the middle of the city of Pittsburgh, it is an oasis with beautiful trees, grazing deer, and wild geese. There are a lot of wild geese! Oftentimes when I walk by a particular pond there will be dozens of geese lazing around. I am always a little bit nervous when I am surrounded by these birds. They don't look at all alarmed as they watch me out of the corner of their stone cold eyes. I get the sense that at any moment they could turn on me and within seconds I would become a pâté for a goose. Every now and then they "honk" at me just to let me know they see me and remind me that it is by their beneficence that I may pass. The truth is, geese are wild and can be dangerous. You think I'm joking? YouTube it. I am pretty much placing my life in their hands each time I walk through their territory. I've learned that when you are dealing with an aggressive goose you are supposed to make eye contact and slowly walk away. Or is it drop to the ground and roll up in a ball? I can never remember. I keep repeating to myself, "Even though I walk through the gaggle of geese I fear no evil for you are at my side."

I have come to realize that the Holy Spirit also often makes people nervous. You can't know what the Spirit is going to do, and this uncertainty can cause anxiety—an anxiety I have felt when walking by live geese. I'm just not sure what they might do next. You see, we like the known and the unknown makes us nervous. The unpredictability of the Spirit often causes us to feel uneasy.

I've long been suspicious that this nervousness has caused us to attempt taming the Holy Spirit. But the Spirit of God cannot be tamed. We try to relegate the wild goose to a wilderness reserve where we can visit and even admire, but this allows us to keep our eye on him. We are okay with the Wild Goose as long as it stays in our very clearly defined boundaries. But we don't really want the Holy Spirit to be loose, don't want it to be too close and certainly don't have any real personal interaction with such a wild bird.

We try to control the Holy Spirit (by trying to live according to our plans, not God's) and forget that the Spirit will blow where the Spirit wills (Jn 3:8). Pope Francis put it this way; "The temptation is always within us to resist the Holy Spirit, because he takes us out of our comfort zone and unsettles us . . . is always easier and more comfortable to settle in our sedentary and unchanging ways. In truth, the Church shows her fidelity to the Holy Spirit in as much as she does not try to control or tame him."[1]

We were never supposed to try to control the Spirit. That is totally backwards; it is the Spirit that is supposed to control us. And because we don't know exactly what that means we engage the Spirit from a safe distance. We don't want to get bit. We like to sing songs about the warmth and the fire of the Holy Spirit but don't really want to be burned. We like the image of the flame of a single candle, but a wild, raging fire frightens us. Our immediate thought is, "Get it under control."

It's really terribly sad. There is a Latin phrase "*corruptio optimi pessima*" that means "the corruption of the best is the worst."

xii   *Breath of God*

Simply put, when we take something that is good and somehow make it bad or use it for corrupt purposes, it is much worse than if the thing were already bad or mediocre.

How did we get to a place where even a single person resists the Spirit of Jesus? Jesus spoke of the Spirit as our comforter, advocate, helper, and the promise of his Father. St. Paul proclaims that "the love of God has been poured out into our hearts through the Holy Spirit that has been given to us" (Rom 5:5). How did the Spirit become a source of fear, confusion, and disunity? How did so many become apathetic to the Holy Spirit? I am aware that we don't all feel this all the time, but at one time or another, most believers do. Whether in spiritual direction, confession or at retreats and conferences I often encounter people who resist the Spirit of God for many of the reasons mentioned. I don't think it should be that way.

As the Holy Spirit is for us, there is an evil spirit, and he is against us. If the evil one can cause us to question the Holy Spirit, to resist the Spirit and not be open to God's Spirit in our life, then we won't seek the Spirit's aid and protection, his peace, his presence, and his anointing. We will seek to live the Christian life without the power of God and will ultimately be ill-equipped to face the struggles that lie before us. Then we will be defeated. *Corruptio optimi pessima.*

It does not have to be that way; it must not be.

Living a life in the Spirit is the ultimate adventure. I can guarantee you will see things you never imagined and go places you never dreamed of. There will be times when you will feel like giving up, but out of nowhere you will be filled with power to keep going. You will fall in love again and again and again. Your heart will be broken and healed and it will be made stronger each time. There will be times when you will feel totally lost, confused, and in the dark and be filled with utter excitement anticipating and wondering how God is going to save the day. You will become an integral part of the most amazing, passionate love affair ever known to humanity. Your life will not be your own, and you won't care. Such is living a life in the Spirit.

Ultimately that is the purpose of this book; to help us to live our life in the Spirit of God. I firmly believe that God desires to be more present to each of our lives and often times we don't appreciate this or recognize it. My prayer is that this book helps us to encounter the Spirit more often and in more ways. Whether it be in the sacraments, the scriptures, prayer, family, work, or while shopping at the local mall, God wants to engage us. Each time we encounter God we have the possibility of being changed, forgiven, restored, filled, and freed. God's breath gives life to our tired spirits.

My prayer for you is that you would be able to fly with the Wild Goose rather than try to run from or tame it. Then and only then will you be truly alive.

1

THE SPIRIT
BREATHES ON US

Jerusalem was all abuzz. The authorities had hoped that getting rid of Jesus would bring a resolution to the tension surrounding him, but it only made things worse. Well, it wasn't really the execution that was causing the problem; it was that pesky rumor of his resurrection from the dead that was the real issue.

The crowds had gathered in Jerusalem and people could feel that something was building, something was about to happen.

St. Luke, who tradition teaches was an artist, paints the scene for us in the second chapter of the Acts of the Apostles.

The scene he paints is, of course, Pentecost.

But perhaps it's best to first take a quick step back to see how we got there. In the first chapter of Acts, Jesus appeared to the apostles after his crucifixion and resurrection. He asked them not to leave Jerusalem. Obviously, things are about to get interesting. Rather than leaving, they are instructed to "wait for the promise of the Father—about which you have heard me speak; for John baptized with water, but in a few days you will be baptized with the Holy Spirit" (Acts 1:5–6).

I am fairly confident that they had no idea what Jesus was talking about. They probably didn't remember the parable where Jesus said, "What father among you would hand his son a snake when he asks for a fish? Or hand him a scorpion when he asks for an egg? If you then, who are wicked, know how to give good gifts to your children, how much more will the Father in heaven give the holy Spirit to those who ask him?" (Lk 11:11–13).

Sure, the first part makes sense. I mean, really, what kind of father would give his son a snake for a fish? But the whole meaning of the "Father in heaven and Holy Spirit" just might have escaped the disciples' understanding.

However, Jesus had mentioned something like that on another occasion. At the end of Luke, he once again makes a similar statement: "And behold I am sending the promise of my Father upon you; but stay in the city until you are clothed with power from on high" (Lk 24:49). Maybe they were beginning to understand, maybe not.

At any rate, Jesus mentions on multiple occasions the promise of the Father. What exactly is the promise of the Father and how will the disciples come to understand?

"Go to Jerusalem and wait," Jesus tells the apostles. It's not hard to imagine a few of the apostles wondering how long they will have to wait, and for what were they waiting.

I wonder what they noticed first. Was it the wind? A noise?

Suddenly, from the sky, from no particular place and from everywhere, there came a strong, driving wind. This evokes familiar scenes of a beach house being battered by hurricane-force winds. One can imagine the noise of the wind rushing through cracks in doors. It must have been chaotic.

"What's going on?"

"What's happening?"

Tongues of fire appear to them, eventually parting and resting on each of them. What must this have looked like? A hovering, massive ball of fire inches above their head?

Really? As if the driving wind wasn't enough a little fire is thrown in for good measure.

The fire appears overhead and then begins to divide, finally resting on each of them. The fire consumes them. The fire, the wind, and the promise of the Father overwhelms them.

Each of the apostles is filled with the Holy Spirit and *all* present were astounded and amazed. Of course they were astounded and amazed; this event would change the history of humanity. It was a spectacular event. The love of the Father and the Son which animated Jesus' life on earth was being poured into the hearts of God's people. God's spirit, his very self, was being shared with his creation, us. This was a startling display of God's power and sovereignty. The Pentecost event in the Acts of the Apostles once again reveals that God chooses to show himself with great power that can astound and amaze crowds.

Sometimes.

BREATH OF GOD

Sometimes God reveals himself and it amazes the crowds. Sometimes it is not as dramatic.

I'm always intrigued when I think and pray about the event of the Acts of the Apostles with the reception of the Holy Spirit found in John's gospel (Jn 20:22). Both events are recounted in the readings at the Liturgy on the Feast of Pentecost.

The account in Luke of the apostles receiving the Holy Spirit is certainly more familiar. The thunder, shaking room, and tongues of fire all make for great stories and homilies. However, I find John's account of the apostles receiving the Holy Spirit equally, if not more, compelling. While the effect is the same—the disciples are empowered—the means by which this happens is remarkably different.

Once again the apostles were all together in one place, in a locked room because they were afraid, terrified perhaps. Let's not lose sight of the paralyzing nature of their fear. Jesus had recently been executed. The one they loved had left the very room they were gathered in and was led to his death—a horrific, public execution. The disciples were very aware of what the mob was capable of doing and did not want to fall under their vengeful wrath. They were hiding because they were afraid that they might be next. There was no indication that the killing was going to stop with Jesus; they didn't know what the religious leaders or Romans were thinking, so they hid. I have never experienced this sort of fear. I was afraid I would get grounded for a bad grade or I feared I would get a ticket for speeding, but I have never feared for my life.

Can you imagine being in a small room, filled with terror that the authorities may find you and, if they did, you could be condemned to die?

I would guess the disciples were being extremely quiet. Every creak caused their hearts to skip a beat.

"Did you hear that?"

"Who is it?"

"Is someone there?"

The scriptures don't say exactly how Jesus appeared, they just state that he did. John simply says that Jesus came and stood in their midst.

The Lord offers them peace, reminding them (and us) that peace is the presence of someone, not merely an absence of something. Jesus' presence and his greeting provide peace in the midst of their fear. He does not cast out the fear the disciples were experiencing, but he rather offers peace. His peace changes them.

Jesus then shows the disciples the wounds in his hands and side. This was to confirm Jesus' identity, to reveal to the disciples that it was really Jesus. Without the wounds they couldn't know for sure.

"It sure looks like Jesus, but Jesus was crucified and this person has no signs of a crucifixion."

On the contrary. Jesus reveals his wounds to those present to let them know it is really him. It's important that Jesus confirms who he is by showing his wounds. It reminds us of the connection between the Cross and the Resurrection; they go together. Jesus had to suffer the agony of death before the beauty of the Resurrection. In the midst of our cross, our wounds, there is always hope. When we are overwhelmed with our difficulties and suffering we recall that this is not the final word. We remember that not even death on a cross could defeat Jesus. The wounded, crucified one is alive!

Jesus, for a second time, offers the disciples peace as if to say, "Don't let the wounds, the suffering rob you of your peace."

He then breathes on them.

Breathing on someone is such a personal gesture. We've all had someone breathe on us. When I was a little kid, breathing on my friends was a part of my morning routine. I recall in second grade each morning I would play a game with a few of the other boys in my class. We would walk up to one another and breathe in each other's face. We would then try to guess what the other had for breakfast. Syrup was always a dead giveaway. The girls would think it was so gross, but I think they were just jealous that we didn't allow them to be a part of our fun. Even as silly as it was, there was a closeness, something personal (and maybe gross) about breathing on one another.

Jesus breathes on the apostles, and that's it. He breathes on them and invites them to "receive the Holy Spirit."

That's all, no driving wind, shaking buildings, or tongues of fire. Just a simple breath, the breath of God. It's an image we see in Genesis where God "blew into the nostrils the breath of life, and the man became a living being" (Gn 2:7). The breath of God, the *ruah*, in Hebrew, brings life to humanity's flesh. Humanity is not truly alive until the breath of God enters us.

I find this a beautiful image. From the dust of the earth God forms humanity and then, in a deeply personal action, God draws humanity close to himself and bringing man's face to his own, God breathes life. God himself breathes life into humanity.

The breath of God rushes throughout all scripture. Job proclaims, "For the spirit of God has made me, and the breath of the Almighty gives me life" (Jb 33:4). In the thirty-seventh chapter of Ezekiel we find a stark image of God showing the prophet Ezekiel a valley of dry bones. The Lord asks Ezekiel if the dry bones can come back to life, to which Ezekiel wisely responds that only the Lord would know such a thing. The Lord instructs Ezekiel to prophesy and breathe life into the bones. Ezekiel does as the Lord commanded and the bones "came to life." The bones rattle, shake and begin to move, much like getting out of bed in the morning, and they come to life. The Lord then reminds Ezekiel that he will put his spirit in him so that he will also come to life (see Ezekiel 37:1–14).

Jesus appeared to the apostles and offered them peace and breathes on them. Jesus breathes life *into* them, not merely on them. The breath of Jesus consumed them; it entered their very beings. The disciples received the breath of Jesus; they breathed in his breath and received his life. The breath of the Spirit changed the disciples.

EXPERIENCES OF THE HOLY SPIRIT ARE OFTEN SIMPLE

One of the reasons I love John's portrayal of the disciples receiving the Holy Spirit is because of the simplicity and subtlety of it. When the disciples receive the Holy Spirit in Acts it is such a dramatic, big scene. The driving wind (breath of God), thunder, and tongues of fire are a familiar image to many of us because we have read and heard this story since our youth. It's a wonderful story that is a key to the life of the Church. But for most people, this is a story they have *heard* but not an encounter they have *experienced*. How many people have experienced such things? Who has experienced the Holy Spirit as a strong, driving wind that shakes a building? I've heard stories of those who have had such experiences, but I think most would agree it is the exception rather than the rule. No doubt Christians long and clamor for such experiences, but the reality is that they are very, very rare.

The account from Acts is wonderful, but more often than not, it hasn't been my experience. That is not to say that I have not experienced the power of God's spirit; on the contrary, but it has rarely been in a manner recounted in the Acts of the Apostles. It is generally much simpler, more gentle and subtle, more like a breath than a strong, driving wind. In that sense it is similar to Elijah's experience; he did not encounter God in the earthquake or the fire but in the gentle breeze (breath of God) (see 1 Kings 19:12).

So often we are a people who both love and have grown to expect spectacles, the bigger the better. Lights, fire, noise—anything that captures our attention and lures us in. I recall attending an indoor soccer game when I was in college. I had been invited to attend by my older brother and I reluctantly accepted. At the time I was not much of a soccer fan; I thought the games were slow and kind of boring. However, I was struck by the orchestrated show before the game commenced. There were explosions, fireworks, smoke, and noise before the match started and it was all extremely engaging. The spectacle was necessary in order to engage the crowd.

In Acts, St. Luke writes that the *crowd* was amazed and astounded by the driving wind and the tongues of fire. Maybe crowds need such things in order to be amazed? Is a breath going to astound a crowd? With St. John there is no driving wind, nor is there a crowd. Rather, only Jesus, peace, wounds, and a breath. Could it be that only disciples and not crowds are able to encounter Jesus and his Spirit in wounds and the subtlety of a breath?

I'm afraid we have often behaved like the crowd expecting brilliant, hypnotizing spectacles that stimulate our senses. At times we want the same from God, and because of this we often miss his simple, transforming breath.

The challenge for us is to be able to perceive the breath of God. The only way this can happen is for us to stay close enough to God that when he breathes we are aware of it. Imagine the closeness of an infant being held to her mother's chest. When either the baby or mother breathes the other is aware. That's how close I want to be to the Lord: the Lord breathes and I am filled.

The Spirit's movement is often subtle; it's essential for us to be aware of this in order to experience the Lord's grace. If we are only looking for the earthquake we will always miss the breath. If I come to experience that the Lord's movement is often found in a breath then I am more likely to encounter the living God.

BREATHE ON ME

Oftentimes it begins with a simple prayer.

"Jesus, come with your Holy Spirit."

Pray that God would breathe life into any doubts you may have. Sometimes I pray and wonder if God even hears me. Many people struggle because they hear stories of the abundant life that others are experiencing and time and time again they seem to come up empty, not really living but merely surviving. Many want to believe that God has more for them but get tired of asking or tired of being disappointed, so they stop asking.

Take a moment and ask God to breathe faith into your heart. Pray that God would breathe power and strength into your weakness. So many people have said to me that they have tried countless times to change things in their lives. And yet, it seems the harder they try the quicker they fall. They often begin to wonder if there really is power over weakness, sinfulness, addictions, and fear.

Pray that at this very moment the Lord would breathe on you. Pray that the heavenly Father would breathe the same life-giving breath that rested on the apostles. The breath that moved frightened followers from a locked room to the corners of the earth. Pray that God would breathe that life into you. Pray that the Father would breathe courage into your fear.

"Jesus your breath of life changed the disciples; may it change me."

Questions for Reflection

1. How do you experience the Holy Spirit as a person?
2. What does it mean to you to have a relationship with the Holy Spirit?

Try This . . .

Take a few minutes where you are free from distractions. Quiet yourself. Take a deep breath and ask the Holy Spirit to come to you.

2
THE SPIRIT IS GENEROUS TO US

When I was a young kid I was helping with some work at the athletic complex where I was an indentured servant. We had to move some bales of straw across a couple of ball fields. Each one weighed about as much as I did. I remember struggling with a bale and my boss standing back watching me.

"Need some help?"

"Nope, I got this."

But it was evident that I didn't; I was in over my head. I kept on trying to pick up the bale and carry it across the field. I tried pushing and pulling but didn't get very far. Eventually my boss said to me, "Are you going to ask for help or let someone help you or are you just going to struggle there by yourself?" It seemed like a silly question because it was quite obvious what I was going to do. I was going to do it by myself. Eventually, after a few more frustrating minutes (or was it hours?) I had to admit what everyone else knew—that I needed help.

"I can do it myself" is a recipe for trouble in the spiritual life.

We need the help of the Holy Spirit. One of the ways God chooses to help us is by providing gifts to aid us in our spiritual life. You remember the gifts, right? The gifts of the Holy Spirit?

"Um . . . the gifts, sure. Ya, the gifts of the Holy Spirit? Remind me, it's been a long time since Confirmation."

Some people have only a vague idea of what the gifts of the Holy Spirit are while others are a little more knowledgeable. There are gifts spoken of in the Old Testament often referred to as the "Old Testament gifts" (catchy) or the "Isaiah gifts" because they are found in the eleventh chapter of Isaiah. There are also the "New Testament gifts" or the "Corinthian gifts" (see 1 Cor 12), also known as the "charismatic gifts."

My experience of discussing the gifts of the Holy Spirit is often met with mixed reactions. When I am dealing with the Old Testament gifts mentioned in Isaiah 11:2–3 (wisdom, understanding, counsel, fortitude, knowledge, piety, and fear of the Lord) most people are pretty receptive to hearing about them. I think lots of Catholics are generally aware of the Old Testament gifts and don't find them to be intimidating or, let's be honest, strange. However, when I start talking about the gifts of the New Testament (1 Cor 12) I often find myself dealing with people who have preconceived opinions that sometimes inhibit them from being fully open to the gifts. This is unfortunate because all of the gifts can aid us in our spiritual life and help us to become holy.

I have heard lots of people say they want to "seek the giver, not the gift" when referring to their hesitation about the gifts of the Holy Spirit. On one level I agree with such a sentiment. I've met people who have made receiving a particular spiritual gift so paramount that they have lost sight of the giver of the gift, God. However, I've also dealt with others who have used such a statement as a way of not being open to the Lord's gifts. I've prayed with men and women who, when asked if they wanted to receive gifts, responded that they really just want to seek the Lord. This is admirable, but seeking the Lord and receiving the Lord's gifts are not mutually exclusive; it is not one or the other. I absolutely want to seek the face of God and long to know him and love him. I also want all of the gifts the Lord desires to impart to me. It's important for us to realize that the gifts actually help us seek the Lord. They help us pray, discern, and listen. Ultimately they help us to be more like Jesus. The gifts do not cause us to lose sight of the Lord, rather they should help us see him more clearly. They should help awaken in us the presence of God.

OLD TESTAMENT

In the Old Testament the spirit is very much connected with life and death. If one has the spirit one has life and without the spirit there is no life. Once again Job makes this clear. "If he were to set his mind to it, gather to himself his spirit and *breath*, all flesh would perish together, and mortals return to dust" (Jb 34:14–15, emphasis added).

The Spirit *gives* life and the gifts of the Spirit help sustain life. I like the image that Fr. Bernhard Blankenhorn, O.P., a professor at the Gregorian University in Rome, uses when speaking of the Old Testament gifts of the Holy Spirit. Fr. Bernhard compares the gifts of the Holy Spirit to a sail on a boat. The breath of God, the wind, is blowing and the gifts are the sails that catch that wind and allow us to move. It is only when the sails fully catch the wind that the soul is able to fully sail.[1]

When I was growing up, my family would often go sailing. Sailing wasn't very popular in Colorado, and to be honest, there were times when I wished we had a speed boat. I enjoyed water skiing and just storming around the lake on an inner tube. But my dad loved sailing. I think his life as a busy physician was already too fast and crazy and he didn't want his entertainment to add to this craziness. He loved the peace and quiet. But for me, at times, there was just too much quiet for my liking. Often in the middle of the day there was little wind, and rather than sailing, we did a lot of floating. My siblings and I would jump out of the boat to swim and play in the water. My dad would sit back, tip his hat over his eyes and just be. Inevitably, the wind would return in the evening and away we went. I must admit, I did grow to enjoy the serenity of evening sailing. But what I adored was when the wind was really strong and both the main sail and the jib sail (the front sail) were so full that the boat would lean and be in danger of tipping. At that point my brothers and I would get to sit on the upper edge of the boat leaning back over the water in order to make sure the boat stayed steady. You could feel the power of the wind in the sails of the boat. There was a connection, a union with the wind. We could manipulate the sails and the direction and speed of the boat would immediately be impacted. At those moments I loved sailing. It was exhilarating. You felt alive.

The experience of God's spirit is similar. He wants to fill our sails so that our spiritual life becomes exhilarating, so we feel alive. I don't think we were meant to sit in the middle of the lake bobbing up and down and getting sea sick. Rather, the Spirit blows and is always blowing—there is no midday lull—and the gifts of the Spirit catch the wind. We are united with the Lord and our soul begins to soar.

There is no definitive statement on exactly how each of the gifts works, how they "catch God's breath." The *Catechism of the Catholic Church* puts it this way: "These are permanent dispositions which make man docile in following the promptings of the Holy Spirit" (CCC 1830). So the gifts of the Holy Spirit are supposed to help us respond to the Spirit of God who is present and always active in the world.

We received these gifts when we were baptized and the gifts are able to grow only if they are used. The opposite is also true; if we fail to use them, they merely flap in the wind. If we ignore our spiritual life the gifts also become less active. It is not that the Holy Spirit is taken away from us, but that merely our ability to experience the fullness of God's gifts is lessened.

Pope Francis has stressed our need to receive the gifts of the Holy Spirit. In the spring of 2014, he took the opportunity to teach extensively on the Old Testament gifts. He stated, "The Spirit himself is 'God's gift' par excellence (cf. John 4:10), a gift from God, and in turn communicates different spiritual gifts to those who welcome him. The Church identifies seven, a number that symbolically speaks of fullness, completeness; we learn these when preparing for the sacrament of Confirmation and we invoke them in the ancient prayer called the 'Sequence of the Holy Spirit' the gifts of the Holy Spirit are: wisdom, understanding, counsel, fortitude, knowledge, piety and fear of God."[2]

Over many weeks the Holy Father taught about each of the gifts. I think it's helpful to keep in mind that the gifts have a practical application to our life. They are not these mysterious magic powers that have no real connection to our lived experience. On the contrary, the gifts become real to us as we experience them in our daily life.

The gift of **wisdom** is often understood to be a gift of someone who is really smart and can figure out complicated or deep issues. While there is a certain truth to that, it is much more. Wisdom is not only a gift of the mind, it also pertains to the heart. Wisdom helps us perceive the realities of our faith and makes our faith more real. Wisdom enlightens our understanding of God and aids us in appropriating God's way of life for us. It helps us discern the things of God from those of the world and assists us in choosing the good. Wisdom allows us to understand and see the beauty of

God which moves our heart to long for him. Pope Francis stated, "This is wisdom: it is the grace of being able to see everything with the eyes of God. It is simply this: seeing the world situations, conjunctures, problems, everything with God's eyes. This is wisdom."[3] The gift of wisdom allows us to see everyday occurrences in the light of grace. When confronted with difficult situations wisdom allows us to get past the greys and shadows and have a clearer understanding about what God may be asking of us.

While the gift is important for all Christians, I would think it is particularly so for parents. Raising children in today's world presents issues never seen before. How does one guide and form children being bombarded by messages from the world through mediums like Facebook, Instagram, and Twitter? Wisdom helps parents sift through that maze and aids them with an ever growing difficult task. Moms and dads, pray for wisdom.

Understanding allows us to perceive the deeper realities of our faith. Everyone has heard that God's love is perfect and unconditional but do we really understand this? On one level we are able to hear about his love, but the gift of understanding moves us from a mere intellectual understanding to a way of knowing this reality that changes our lives. It is not just "understanding" that God loves us, but understanding that his love is enough to satisfy us. A person with the gift of understanding is more rooted in her faith; therefore, her faith is not merely a list of doctrinal facts that have been memorized.

When we are moved to a deeper level of understanding, that impacts how we treat people. If, in the depths of who I am, I have experienced the love of God, this motivates me, enables me to love more. If I have been profoundly affected by God's forgiveness I will become more forgiving. Pope Francis puts it this way, "understanding is a grace that only the Holy Spirit can infuse and which awakens in the Christian the ability to go beyond the outward appearance of reality and scrutinize the depths of God's thoughts and His plan of salvation. This is a beautiful gift that the Lord has given us all. It is the gift with which the Holy Spirit brings us into intimacy with God and makes us part of the plan of love that he is weaving into the plots of our lives and history. It helps us to understand the true meaning of history."[4]

Perhaps one of the clearest examples of the gift of understanding came from a cousin of mine who was about eight years old. When celebrating Mass and reflecting on the scripture where Jesus said, "let the children come to me" (Mt 19:14), I asked why Jesus may have said this. My cousin Becky stated, "Maybe it's because big people complicate God, and he is not so complicated." The homily quickly ended given that there was nothing I could add to such a beautiful statement. Understanding allows us to see and comprehend God who is not that complicated.

Counsel gives us graced insight into the movement of God in our lives. The gift of counsel allows us clarity as we move forward in discerning God's will and direction in our life. Pope Francis states, "This is the gift with which the Holy Spirit helps us to make decisions in our concrete lives . . . God enlightens our hearts and directs our thoughts, words, and actions in accordance with his saving will."[5]

Most often when people come to me for spiritual direction they want to know what God is asking of them. The way I approach spiritual direction is I seek to help the person to see what God is doing in his or her life. God is present and active and wants to lead and direct us but oftentimes we don't recognize it. We often ask questions such as: Should I change jobs? Should we move? What do I need to do in order to grown closer to God? These are questions I get from people all the time and the gift of counsel can be a tremendous blessing for such questions. So often we try to make decision according to our own wants, desires, or intuition, and this often leads to poor results. The gift of counsel helps us to do what God asks of us.

It's important that we realize that this gift is not only for those huge life decisions. Rather, God wants to direct our actions in lots of ways. I remember one time a spiritual director of mine challenged me to respond to any "nudge of the Spirit." What exactly is a "nudge of the Spirit" I wondered. It was not a theological term with which I was familiar. I came to realize a "nudge" is often a small sense or feeling that God wants to get my attention about something. What I realized was that God would bring people or situations to my mind and heart and often times I would dismiss them. The more I prayed I realized that he was inviting me to act on those thoughts or feelings. The question then was what should I do? Sometimes I would simply pray for the person, while other times I might send them a text message reminding them that they are loved and that I was praying for them. This very simple gesture is often received with great gratitude. So often when I do this I get a response from the person telling me how much they appreciated and needed what I said. When I am able to respond in this manner it confirms for me that God is always active in our lives and wants to make us more aware of this.

The gift of **fortitude** allows us to move forward in doing what is right and good. Often times we know (by the gift of counsel) what we should do but we lack the power (fortitude) to do it. This gift provides the grace necessary to boldly speak (or be silent) and act when necessary. Fortitude is said to be the gift for martyrs because it strengthens them to be faithful to God even unto death. However, I think it is also absolutely necessary for daily Christian living. Jesus says we need to pick up our cross daily (Lk 9:23); often I find this is terribly difficult. It is usually the little, daily inconveniences with which I struggle. Some days I just don't feel like trying; I am tired and feel like giving up. I need help not only in the heroic things but in the mundane tasks of life. The Holy Father states: "Through the gift of fortitude, we receive the strength to do God's will in spite of our own natural weakness and limitations . . . For most of us, the gift of fortitude is exercised in our patient pursuit of holiness in the circumstances of our daily lives. Whenever we feel weary or discouraged along the journey of faith, let us ask the Holy Spirit to grant us the gift of fortitude, to refresh us."[6]

Left to my own strength I am just not strong enough to be the person God wants me to be or for that matter, the person I want to be. Time and time again I make decisions about things I want to do or don't want to do. Without the gift of fortitude I am sure to fall. (Truth be told, even with the gift of fortitude I occasionally fall.) Discipline and stubbornness can only get us so far. In fact, this is something that actually causes a lot of people great grief and stress. They share with me that in so many areas of their life they are very disciplined. "But, I can't seem to shut up when we all start complaining about our boss." We have bought into a lie that says if we only try harder we can be more Godly, and this is not true and leads to confusion, frustration, and in extreme cases, despair. We can't do this on our own power. We need the gift of fortitude in order to do what we know is right.

Knowledge? Wisdom? Understanding? Aren't they all the same? Actually, no they aren't. Knowledge helps us see things the way God sees them. It casts light on matters of faith and aids in our belief and understanding. Pope Francis put it this way, "The gift of knowledge puts us in tune with God's gaze on things and on people . . . Through this spiritual gift, we are enabled to see every person, and the world around us, in the light of God's loving plan."[7]

I often pray, "Lord, let me see things the way you do." The reality is that I am pretty much blind. Well, maybe not totally blind, but it may actually be better if I were. If I were totally blind I would be aware of my inability to see. However, given that I have some sight I think I can see fine and am often not aware of the blind spots in my life. I know that oftentimes the way I see people and situations is hampered by my fear, prejudice, insecurity, and weakness. I need God's gift of wisdom to see things more like he does. The gift of knowledge helps me to understand why I do what I do. It helps me to know what is God's spirit moving in my life and what are my own inclinations. Sometimes that may actually be the same, but at times they are not. I need to know.

Piety is the gift that spurs us on to worship God for his greatness. With the gift of piety we receive a desire to serve the Lord not only out of duty, but out of a deep love and reverence for God. Pope Francis stated, "Piety is not mere outward religiosity; it is that genuine religious spirit which makes us turn to the Father as his children and to grow in our love for others, seeing them as our brothers and sisters, members of God's family."[8]

Once again, we can't just make things happen in the spiritual life. Yes, we need to do our part, we must engage the will and the intellect. We also need to make ourselves available to God and his grace in order to give God the worship he deserves. Left to my own power I am unable to worship God and therefore I need the gift of piety.

How many times have you gone to Mass and at the end of the liturgy been surprised by that fact that you got absolutely nothing out of the liturgy? Your mind was so distracted by any number of things that you were not able to enter into the Mass. Or have you ever tried to mediate on the mysteries of the Rosary and find yourself in the fourth mystery wondering how you got there? We often tell ourselves that we need to be more focused, we need to try harder to pay attention. What we really need is to be more intentional about asking for the gift of piety. If we are going to worship the way God intends we need to be intentional about asking for God's gifts so that the Spirit of God moves in us.

It is then that we are able pray and worship in God's power and not our own.

Fear of the Lord is not really what it sounds like. God is madly in love with us and we need not fear him like we fear the dark. Rather, fear of the Lord is connected to the virtue of hope. We are fully aware that no matter what happens God is faithful and he will never leave us. Fear of the Lord enables us to have a confidence in God's love for us and a deep desire never to offend that love. It also creates in us a confidence in God's grace to sustain us in our walk with God. Pope Francis puts it this way: "The fear of the Lord is the gift of the Holy Spirit through whom we are reminded of how small we are before God and of his love and that our good lies in humble, respectful and trusting self-abandonment into his hands. This is fear of the Lord: abandonment in the goodness of our Father who loves us so much."[9]

More than once I had to take the long, lonely, frightening walk from the classroom to the principal's office. It could have been for any number of personal indiscretions that seemed so prevalent at the time. I remember one particular time being invited to leave my accounting class due to a surprisingly boisterous outburst. I recall walking down the hallway thinking, "OK, that was stupid. You've really done it this time." On the trek to the administrative office I thought of the various punishments which might be coming my way. While I couldn't recall the last time a student was publicly flogged I did not rule out the possibility that it might be my punishment.

We often approach the Lord in the same manner. We are riddled with fear that we will get the punishment we deserve. However, we are not focusing on God's love and mercy at moments such as this; rather, we are looking at our failings and approaching God out of fear rather than love. The gift of fear of the Lord allows us to approach God, to walk down that long, lonely hallway, pursuing God who is madly in love with us and will be running to greet us and welcome us home.

We limit what God can do in our lives because we don't continually seek and ask for the gifts of the Holy Spirit. To return to the sailing analogy, at times we get frustrated that our boat is not going anywhere. But upon further inspection we realize that we failed to put up the sails. We sit in the middle of the lake wondering why we never get anywhere, why we don't seem to grow and move forward. All along it was because our sails had not been filled. Slowly, let's put up our sails, by praying for the gifts of the Holy Spirit, and let the breath of God catch them. Then, and only then, can we ever move forward and experience the joy and excitement of living a life moved by the Spirit of God.

Questions for Reflection

1. What Old Testament gift of the Holy Spirit do you most desire and why?

2. Pope Francis states the Spirit is the gift. How do you receive the Spirit as *the* gift?

Try This . . .

Admit to the Lord that too often you try to captain the ship that is your life. Take a moment and give the Holy Spirit permission to be in charge of your life.

3
THE SPIRIT GIVES US GIFTS

Not only is the Holy Spirit generous in the ways we learned in the last chapter, but he desires to give us even more gifts. The Old Testament gifts are easier to talk about; there are seven, and while at times it's easy to get them a bit mixed up, they are pretty straightforward and nothing is terribly "odd" about them. The New Testament gifts? Well, that's a whole different story.

The New Testament gifts, often called the charismatic gifts, are not as identifiable. It's not as clear how many gifts there are, and the gifts are mentioned throughout much of the New Testament. In several different places St. Paul writes about the gifts of the Spirit; his letter to the Corinthians is the most well-known.

DEFINING "CHARISMATIC"

Now may be a good time to deal with the charismatic elephant in the room. Oftentimes when people hear talk of the Holy Spirit, their minds automatically think of the word, "charismatic," and for some of those same people, this causes a degree of anxiety. This is unfortunate because occasionally, this sort of anxiety can close a person to the grace of the Holy Spirit. Some Catholics are under the false asssumption that all "Holy Spirit talk" is actually code for "the Charismatic Renewal" (a graced movement in the Church that we'll discuss in further detail soon), and therefore, any mention of the Holy Spirit causes them to be suspicious. Because of this they may not be as open to learning about the third person of the Trinity as they may normally be. For this reason, I think it's important to distinguish between the Holy Spirit, the charismatic gifts, and the Charismatic Renewal as a movement in the Church.

The word "charismatic" simply means "charisms" or "gift or grace." It's not a gift we receive for doing a good job or because we have behaved; rather, it's a gift that helps our ability to actually be good. The grace helps us live the Christian life that God intended. With that being said, the reality is that the word "charismatic" implies a lot more than that in our culture, attracting some people while repelling others. That means we need to define it in order to understand the Holy Spirit. In the broadest sense, the word "charismatic" means openness to grace.

In this vein, the Church is charismatic. It is in its nature to be open to the Holy Spirit and the Spirit's gifts, and for this reason, the Church can rightly, actually must rightly, be called charismatic. The Charismatic Renewal is an international movement in the Catholic Church which began in the United States in the late, 1960s.

A MOVEMENT OF GRACE

Historically, the Church has been blessed with various movements. These movements distinguish themselves by their ministry and spirituality. They exist to serve the Church and develop the faith and spiritual lives of its members. The Charismatic Renewal is such a movement.

The renewal movement started among a group of university students attending Duquesne in 1967. It has seen fantastic growth with estimates stating that as many as 120 million Catholics from more than two hundred and thirty-five different countries have had some involvement with the Charismatic Renewal.[1] It is difficult to quantify, though, because the renewal is experienced differently in various counties. Also, contrary to popular belief, there is not a secret handshake or a special membership card that distinguishes exactly who is involved in the Renewal.

Key elements of the Charismatic Renewal are the experience of baptism in the Holy Spirit (which we will discuss in chapter five), personal commitment to Jesus, Life in the Spirit Seminar (a retreat focusing on the role of the Holy Spirit in one's life), charismatic retreats, prayer for healing, and prayer meetings with praise and worship that encourage the use of the charismatic gifts, with the gift of tongues being one of the most common. All the popes since Blessed Paul VI to Pope Francis have welcomed groups associated with the Charismatic Renewal.

In the spring of 2014 Pope Francis addressed an international gathering of those involved in the Charismatic Renewal. He thanked them for the gift that they are to the Church, and the Holy Father challenged those gathered not to "cage the Holy Spirit" and to "never lose the freedom that the Holy Spirit gives us." He also exhorted them not to try to control the Holy Spirit. "You are dispensers of God's grace, not controllers!"[2]

Pope Francis also shared how in the past he struggled with the renewal. He stated that there were some elements that he did not appreciate. However, over time and as he met more people involved in the renewal, he realized that the movement was a gift to the Church and had a great deal to offer.

The renewal has been a gift to me. I have been involved in the renewal for about thirty years, and it has been a great blessing in

my life. Many of the people who were in the renewal were tremendous examples of men and women of faith, and they invited
me into a deeper relationship with Jesus than I had ever known.
They also introduced me to a more personal relationship with the
Holy Spirit that gave me the grace and power to actually live my
relationship with Jesus. Over the years I've helped with charismatic retreats and conferences, attended various prayer groups, and
served for a number of years with the National Service Committee,
a national board that serves charismatic groups.

While I have been blessed by my involvement with the
renewal, I am aware that this is not everyone's experience. Pope
Francis is not alone in his initial leeriness toward the renewal.
Over the years I have met numerous people with similar feelings.
My experience is that for the vast majority of people who have
negative feelings toward the renewal, the feelings were caused by
negative interactions with individuals involved in the renewal. This
is unfortunate but true. There is no doubt that some individuals
have made mistakes. Some have been overly zealous and lacked
tact and discernment in their relations with others. It's a shame
that things such as this happen but they do.

Other people have been turned off to the renewal because
they may not have been comfortable with the type of prayer or
music associated with the movement. Or for some it may be the
gift of tongues that bothered them. Here's the thing: for those
negatively impacted, it's important to separate the Holy Spirit, the
third person of the Trinity, from the movement or an individual or
groups of individuals involved in the movement. I've met many
people who have closed themselves to the working of the Holy
Spirit because of negative experiences with individuals involved
in the renewal. We can't be closed to the Holy Spirit. If we are,
we miss the grace that God wants to give us. Being open to God's
Spirit does not mean one is signing up to be a part of a movement.

Rather, one is inviting God to be more present in one's life which is always a good idea.

THE CHURCH AS CHARISMATIC

I remember giving a talk to a group of people who were not exactly open to the Charismatic Renewal. Truthfully, that would be an understatement; a submarine commander would be more open to leaks than this group was to the Charismatic Renewal. Near the beginning of the talk I stated that the Church was by her nature charismatic. An individual a few feet in front of me to my left literally scoffed in an audible manner. You could then hear him say to his companion, "How can he say that?"

Actually, it's not me; it's the Church. The Fathers of the Second Vatican Council wrote a document on the Church titled *Lumen Gentium* (Light to the World) in which they stated this. The Fathers wrote, "The Church, which the Spirit guides in way of all truth and which He unified in communion and in works of ministry, He both equips and directs with hierarchical and charismatics gifts and adorns with his fruits" (LG 4).

The hierarchical aspect is obvious. The structure and order of the Church makes sense, and I can't imagine anyone denying that there is a hierarchical element to the Church. I would also suspect most would agree that the hierarchy is necessary. Sure, at times it may frustrate us, but it would be hard to imagine the Catholic Church (or any organization) without some type of hierarchical order.

In this statement the Church is affirming that she, the hierarchy, is open to and led by the Spirit. "The Church, *which the Spirit guides*" (emphasis mine) is the movement of the Holy Spirit that has continually given guidance to the Church. The Church, laity, religious, priests, and bishops must be open to the Spirit so that she may remain the spotless bride of Christ. It is impossible for the Church to say "no" to the Spirit of God.

The Fathers also went on to say, "It is not only through the sacraments and Church ministries that the same Holy Spirit sanctifies and leads the people of God. He distributes special graces among the faithful of every rank . . . 'the manifestation of the Spirit is given to everyone for profit' (1 Cor 12:7). These charismatic gifts, whether they be the most outstanding or the more simple and widely diffused, are to be received with thanksgiving and consolation, for they are exceedingly suitable and useful for the needs of the Church" (LG 12).

It's beneficial to remember that the Spirit sanctifies and leads "the people of God . . . the faithful of every rank . . . given to everyone." The gifts are not for a select few; rather, they are "widely diffused" and should be "received with thanksgiving." What a beautifully simple statement on the gifts! The Council Fathers are speaking to each of us. The gifts are not only for "them" but they are also for "us."

St. John Paul II wrote, "Indeed, the Church is directed and guided by the Holy Spirit, who lavishes diverse hierarchical and charismatic gifts on all the baptized, calling them to be, each in an individual way, active and co-responsible" (*Christifideles Laici* 21).

Most recently, Pope Francis stated the Holy Spirit "brings forth different charisms which enrich the people of God"[3] The Council Fathers as well as recent popes have all encouraged the Church to receive and embrace the charismatic element of the Church. Now, let's look more closely at the Charismatic gifts.

BEING OPEN TO THE GIFTS

When the conversation of the New Testament gifts is broached, the gift of tongues is often a source of tension and anxiety. My experience is that for some people the gift of tongues is a type of deal-breaker when it comes to openness and receptivity to the gifts of the Holy Spirit. Many, many times people have said to me when praying for the gifts of the Holy Spirit, "OK, let's pray for the Holy Spirit, but I don't want to pray for tongues." When asked why, the answer generally doesn't make a lot of sense and boils down to a few things: either they don't understand it, they find it weird, and/or they don't think they really need it. I will do my best to deal with these issues, but the fact will probably remain that there are some people who simply are not open to the Holy Spirit working in this manner. As is the case with all gifts, your openness to receiving them is up to you. God is not going to force anything on you. I have had someone say to me that they were afraid that if they received the gift of tongues they thought it may start and they would not be able to stop it, as if they would be at the drive-thru at Taco Bell ordering their double decker taco and break out with the gift of tongues unable to finish the order. This will not happen.

With that being said, I don't believe standing before the Lord in a closed posture is something we should knowingly choose to adopt. Not ever. For any reason. My prayer is that I will always go before the Lord open rather than closed. "Lord, what do you want? That's what I want, too."

Let's first keep the gift in perspective. The gift of tongues is not the end-all of the gifts of the Holy Spirit. One does not have to receive the gift in order to go to heaven. Also, we need to remember that without love those who pray in tongues are a clanging gong (1 Cor 13:1). But it is also not an insignificant gift. In the New Testament there are many references made to this gift (Acts 2; Acts 10:46; Acts 19:6; 1 Corinthians 12–14; Romans 8:26; and Jude 1:20 to name a few) and it would probably be wise for us to pay attention and not simply dismiss it as unimportant or "not for me." The gift helps us to pray and helps us experience union with God. I particularly like what St. Paul says in Romans, "the Spirit too comes to the aid of our weakness; for we do not know how to pray as we ought, but the Spirit itself intercedes with inexpressible groanings" (Rom 8:26). This is key for me. At times I simply don't know how to pray. Occasionally when I am interceding for others I don't know what they need and don't know how to pray for them. While at other times noise and confusion so dominate my mind and heart that I don't know what to say. I sit before God in my weakness and silence and I don't know how to pray; I don't know what to say. At those moments I invite the Spirit to pray through me and I experience God. For me there is a letting go and element of surrender that I find freeing. I don't need to "get it right," nor do I need to have a concern about how to pray—I simply let God's Spirit pray through me. "Lord, you know better than I. Teach me to pray."

SO MANY GIFTS

Allowing the Spirit to pray through us also seems to make us more available or open to other gifts of God. The New Testament has many instances where these gifts are mentioned. In 1 Corinthians 12, St. Paul writes extensively about the gifts of the Holy Spirit. He identifies wisdom, knowledge, faith, healing, mighty deeds, prophecy, discernment of spirits, tongues, interpretation of tongues. And then later, he also lists mighty deeds, gifts of healing, assistance, administration, and varieties of tongues. Paul also mentions spiritual gifts in Romans 12:6–8 and Ephesians 4:11. This is not a complete listing of Paul's treatment of the spiritual gifts but only to make mention that he addresses them in several places.

The New Testament gifts are special graces given to individuals in the Church for the building of the Church. The gifts are not to be stored up as personal prizes but are to be shared with the community of faith. In fact, a particular gift does not mean the individual has a greater level of sanctity or holiness; it does not make the person a better Christian or Catholic. It's merely a gift given that if exercised properly may benefit a community of faith. The legitimacy of the gifts should be discerned by the community and only after the gift is affirmed by spiritually mature leaders should it be shared with the community (1 Jn 4:1). Most often the gifts of the Holy Spirit build up the faith of those present. Whether it be a word of encouragement or a prophetic word (a word or insight from the Lord that may give direction to the community), the people of God benefit from what is spoken and the gifts should stir one's faith.

I have seen extraordinary things that have definitely stirred my faith. I have been blessed to be able to participate in and witness to God doing miraculous things. I have been with people who have been healed of painful arthritis, bad backs, hips, hearing and sight issues, deformities of limbs, constant migraines as well as many other infirmities. The people who experienced these healings were obviously blessed but so were those who witnessed them, and this is important to bear in mind. The charismatic gifts are meant to increase people's faith in God. God is the one who gives the gift and God is the one who heals. God is also glorified by those who are healed as well as those who were able to witness God's power.

So often times the real struggle is not necessarily with a particular gift but a question of faith.

Do you believe?

Do you have the faith that God wants to bless us with his gifts? Do you believe God can still work miracles?

Time and time again in the scripture we hear of Jesus not being able to work many miracles due to the lack of people's faith (Mt 13:58; Mk 6:5). Do you believe that Jesus can heal in the world today? Sure, we believe that he did wonderful things in the past. We may also believe that in the past God used many saints to perform mighty deeds, but he really doesn't do that kind of thing today. It's the chicken-and-the-egg dilemma. If we see miracles we may have more faith; but perhaps if we had more faith we would see more miracles. This is key—we ought not to forget to continually ask the Lord for more faith.

There is no doubt in my mind and heart that God can work in physical healings. I have seen too much to ever question that. While this is remarkable, so is the healing that God does in the hearts of those open to yielding to his grace. Through words of knowledge (insights into people's life that are revealed by God), many people experience God's powerful healing presence. I am always amazed that God chooses to use us to help bring freedom to people who have been bound in cycles of pain, guilt, regret, anger, and addiction.

I remember when I was young and just learning about the gifts of the Holy Spirit. It was a beautiful spring day in Minnesota, and I was sitting by a lake with a group of friends. We were hanging out rejoicing that the long winter was over. We began to talk about how we were looking forward to a prayer meeting we were going to attend that evening. While we were chatting, a blind man from my parish, Albert, came to my mind. Albert was probably in his mid-fifties. I had never really met him, but I knew who he was. He was kind of hard to miss and everyone "knew" Albert.

Try as I might, I could not get Albert out of my mind. I figured that I was supposed to pray for him, which I did. However, when I started praying for him, the thought of "second grade" flooded my mind. I didn't know what it meant, but I had a sense that something significant had happened to Albert when he was in second grade. A sense? What do I mean by that? It's hard to explain, but it's like a feeling, or intuition, an insight given by God. The thought comes to my mind and I can't shake it. A friend of mind explains it as "an itch that has to be scratched." I didn't know whether or not Albert would be at the prayer meeting so I didn't give the situation a lot more thought.

As it turned out, Albert did show up to the prayer meeting. I didn't really know what I should do so I quietly prayed for him. Then out of the blue a guy sitting next to me blurted out "I think we are supposed to pray for Albert." He showed me the story in his bible where Jesus had healed the blind man and said, "We need to pray with Albert." He had no idea what was going on in my mind and heart, so I proceeded to share with him how Albert had been on my heart. It was pretty clear to me that God was doing something, and we decided that we should ask Albert if we could pray with him. We approached him and told him that we thought God wanted us to pray with him. Praying *with* others is something else that many people are not familiar with or comfortable with. We will pray *for* someone but are less likely to pray *with* someone. This is too bad because so often praying with someone is such a beautiful experience. Also, it's often the only way we are going to be able to see God work. In the New Testament there are many examples of members of the early Church laying hands on each other and praying (Acts 8:17; 9:17; 19:6; 2 Tm 1:6).

At any rate, Albert was very happy to let us pray and we began. We prayed that God would heal his blindness and his sight would be restored. Nothing was happening so we prayed more fervently and then . . . nothing.

While praying I continued to have the thought of second grade running through my mind. This was all new to me and wasn't totally sure what to do. Finally I said, "Albert, you have been on my mind much of the day. I know we haven't really met, but I keep thinking about second grade. Like, something happened in second grade." Albert looked surprised and was quiet for an extended moment and then became emotional. He went on to explain that he was from a small town and his being blind was just a part of life. Everyone accepted it and worked with it, it just wasn't a big deal—until second grade. He shared that in the second grade the teacher said she didn't know how to teach a person who was blind and that Albert should be in a special school. Albert went on to explain that it was the first time he felt disabled, different, and not totally accepted. It was the first time that he felt defined by his disability or limitation and that it had had a profound impact on him.

In some ways that event changed the trajectory of his life. He eventually had to withdraw from the school to receive more specialized education. He explained that he had harbored anger and frustration for the teacher and the situation. Albert and I spent the next several minutes praying and seeking God's healing. He forgave the teacher for what had happened and then began to share lots of other experiences where he had felt marginalized and hurt. Step by step we walked through numerous hurts and prayed that God would heal him. Slowly we could see the weights being lifted that Albert had been carrying for a long time. This was not the first time that Albert had been prayed with. In fact, many people had prayed with him in the past, but the prayer was always that his sight would be restored. This prayer was different; it was that he would be healed. And he was.

Perhaps it isn't as simple as I think it is, but for me it all comes down to God wanting to give us his gifts so that our faith may increase, we may be healed, and God can be glorified. I think God wants to use all of us. Sure, different people will have different gifts, but all of us are gifted. In the Body of Christ, the Church, there are tremendous gifts present and some people are not even aware of this. I believe God wants to call forth gifts from his people in a very natural and simple way.

When I am speaking at retreats and conferences I often lead everyone in a prayer. I ask each individual to invite the Holy Spirit into his or her heart; pray that God would fill them. Once each person has prayed for the Holy Spirit I then invite them to pray with someone else. The Spirit of God wants to move through us. We are not supposed to be vessels that only store God's Spirit; we are vessels through which the Spirit flows. I help the people to pray with those around them. I try to make it as simple as possible. I invite them to place their hand on the shoulder of someone near them and ask God to bless them. This simple exercise has produced great blessing. It empowers the people present.

There is a tendency to look only to "other people" (the priests, religious, leaders, speakers) as those gifted by God. I believe there is an ocean of untapped grace in the people of God, and if that grace is called forth, grace flows abundantly. When I am praying with a group, I affirm the gifts of the Spirit present in them and then I invite the people to pray that God would bless and heal the person with whom they are praying. Each and every time I do this people are affected; both those praying and those being prayed with. I often hear stories of God healing, restoring, bringing peace and forgiveness to the one being prayed for. I also hear people tell me that they felt God moving through them as they prayed with their brothers and sisters. It's so true. We are blessed when people pray with us, and we are blessed when we pray with others.

Here is a little challenge and invitation for you: the next time someone says to you, "Will you pray for me?" instead of just saying, "Sure!" and then walking away, ask if you can pray right then. Just stop, if it seems appropriate place your hand on his or her shoulder or take his or her hand, and pray. It will maybe take thirty seconds, and I know you will be blessed by the experience.

One of my favorite images of St. Francis has him standing before Jesus with his arms wide open. He is vulnerable and he is open. I want that to always be the manner in which I approach God. It's about God and what he wants to do in and through you and me. I don't think we can approach the Lord with a list of conditions and qualifications. Rather, we approach him as a blank slate and invite him to make something beautiful. Then we step back and watch the Master work.

Questions for Reflection

1. What might be some blocks in your life that inhibit your receiving the Holy Spirit?

2. What are examples of times that you have seen the Holy Spirit work?

Try This . . .

Take a moment or two by yourself. Once you are quiet, pray, "Lord, I don't totally understand, but I want what you want for me. Come Holy Spirit, you are welcome here."

4

THE SPIRIT PRODUCES FRUIT IN OUR LIVES

Jesus says in Matthew that we will be known by our fruit (Mt 7:20). In a very strange event while driving in Austria I discovered what this might mean. I was driving through a lovely manicured village and came upon a group of school children and a police officer standing on the side of the road. Behind the police officer was a display screen that stated I was driving thirty-seven kilometers per hour; the limit was thirty-five, so I wasn't really worried. To my surprise the police officer motioned me to pull over and I immediately began worrying. Being pulled over by the police is a nerve-wracking experience in any setting, but in a foreign country it is even worse. I was concerned about how I was going to communicate to the officer given my German wasn't great. Let's be honest, I didn't actually have any German-speaking abilities. Thank the Lord that I had another priest with me who spoke German pretty well and would be able to help me.

The officer approached my car with two small school children dressed in traditional matching outfits. In the hands of one of the small girls was a large lemon. As the officer approached, I rolled down my window and greeted him with the best German I knew: "Grüß Gott" ("God greet you"). The officer proceeded to receive the lemon from the little girl and handed it to me. He then began speaking to me in German. Apparently, the two words I spoke were so flawless that the officer mistook me for a native. At any rate, I interrupted and explained that I had exhausted my German with the greeting and that I did not understand anything he was saying. The priest with me explained that I did not speak German. The officer hesitated and then chuckled. I think he recognized the humor of the situation. He then went on to explain that the village was trying to raise drivers' awareness about their driving speed. Everyone driving through the village that morning was stopped by the police. If they were driving under the speed limit, they would receive a beautiful, sweet orange from the children. If they were over the limit, even by two measly kilometers per hour, the driver would be stuck with a lemon. I received a sour lemon and it left a lasting impression on me: I will be known by my fruit.

Whether we are aware of it or not, our lives are constantly producing fruit for which we will be known. I recall my parents' fiftieth wedding anniversary attended by my four brothers, my sister, their fifteen grandsons, four granddaughters, one great-granddaughter (hard to get a girl in my family), and countless others whose lives have been impacted by my mom and dad. I preached about the fruit produced from their "I do" fifty years earlier. My parents' yes to the Lord and each other has produced beautiful fruit that is concrete and can be seen.

SPIRITUAL FRUIT

Children and grandchildren are a concrete, visible sign of fruit in my parents' lives. Obviously, it's not only my parents—we all are producing fruit that can be seen. However, we rarely take the time to reflect and think about the type of fruit our lives are producing. This is unfortunate because our spiritual well-being is directly related to the type of fruit we produce. Some fruit is good and some is not but we need to be aware that our lives are producing fruit each and every day. I suppose the question we need to ask is if the fruit we produce is ripe or spoiled. Is it a sweet orange or a sour lemon?

In Galatians, St. Paul writes about the difference between good and bad fruit; fruit of the flesh versus fruit of the Spirit. It's significant that we give reflection to this. The fruit our lives produce can be seen and the fruit our life produces impacts everyone from our mailman, grocery clerk, friends, children, and spouse. If you are known by your fruit, then what do people know about you?

Also, our fruit can be a type of measure for our spiritual growth.

Often people come to me feeling stuck in in their faith life and don't feel like they are making any progress. I often ask them how one measures spiritual growth and progress.

"Is there an app for that?"

"Is there something that allows you to take your spiritual temperature or measures your growth?"

"A divine dipstick?"

One of the ways we can determine if we are growing in the spiritual life is by the fruit. I begin by asking them about the type of fruit their spiritual life is producing.

If you want to see how you are growing in the spiritual life or determine "how you are doing" take a look at the fruit of your life. Is your life producing more fruit of the flesh or of the Spirit? The

two are radically opposed to each other and only that of the Spirit
leads us closer to God.

St. Paul writes that the desires of the flesh are opposed to
those of the Spirit (Gal 5:18). Anyone who has ever tried to diet,
exercise, or go to a movie without consuming a trough of pop-
corn knows this to be true. "Why do I do the things I don't want
to do and don't do the things that I want?" (see Romans 7). We
all live with this tension. The flesh, the body, has desires; some of
them are good and necessary such as the desire for nourishment or
food. When St. Paul is addressing the desires of the flesh this isn't
the type of which he speaks. Rather, the desires of the flesh are
destructive, disordered, and ultimately lead us away from Christ.
Paul says very clearly that the desires of the flesh are against those
of the Spirit and the ability to recognize this conflict is God's grace.

For some people, just realizing that there is this tension, or
this battle between the flesh and the Spirit, is transformative. This
tension that exists between the Spirit and the flesh is just that, a
tension. I've met people who think that if they were holy enough
they would not have to deal with this tension or any temptation.
The truth is that the tension one experiences does not mean that a
person is bad or not seeking God. Simply because we have desires
that seem to be at odds with God's will does not make us bad. It
only brings into light the struggle in which we find ourselves. How
we respond to these desires: now, that's the issue!

FRUIT OF THE FLESH

St. Paul writes that if we are living according to the desires of the
flesh, then the fruits will be destructive. "Now the works of the
flesh are obvious: immorality, impurity, licentiousness, idolatry,
sorcery, hatred, rivalry, jealousy, outbursts of fury, acts of selfishness, dissensions, factions, envy, drinking bouts, orgies, and the like"

(Gal 5:19–21). I've never really been a list person, but this is a list I take seriously.

Try asking yourself these questions to figure out what type of fruit you are producing:

- Am I living my life according to the flesh?
- Are there areas in my life that are dominated by the flesh?

Try imagining what a life dominated by the flesh would actually look like. Simply put, it would be impure. Speech, actions, and thoughts would all smack of licentiousness—an existence lacking any restraint. Whether it be how we eat, drink, or act, a life of licentiousness is always seeking more and going after pleasure with a blatant disregard for the needs of others. This often leads to doing everything in excess. It basically involves doing whatever we want, whenever we want without regard for others or our responsibilities.

If we are living according to the flesh we would produce selfishness, thinking mostly about ourselves, our wants, and our desires. We may every now and then do something for others, but generally service is on our terms, doing what we want when we want.

A life living according to the flesh would be marked with impatience. Impatience with self, family, colleagues, traffic, friends, parishioners, and the people in front of us in line at the grocery store. One would be prone to anger and bursts of yelling.

Fruits of the flesh makes it hard to get along with other people. Sure, we may have a few friends and they would be a lot like us. Our friends would largely think the way we do and continually remind us how right we are. The rest of the world is full of "all those people" who are just dumb, wrong, strange, or different. *They* would drive us crazy, not because something is wrong with us, but because *they* are weird.

We would never be happy or content with what we have. We would always be looking at what everyone else has and making comparisons. Often times we come out "on top" but every now and then we don't and this often leads to those outbursts mentioned earlier. We generally aren't happy with what we have and always want more of what others possess.

St. Paul made a strong claim about those who live according to the flesh: "I warn you, as I warned you before, that those who do such things will not inherit the kingdom of God" (Gal 5:21). Alright, then. No mincing words there. It seems imperative that we reflect on that if for only a moment. St. Paul isn't talking about merely bad habits that may be an annoyance to others. He isn't talking about a bad day that can cause us to be grumpy. No, what St. Paul is talking about is consistent behavior that is so serious that it runs the risk of eternally separating us from the Lord. "I warn you . . . will not inherit the kingdom of God."

I can hear it now because I have heard it so many times before. "Really? But it's just a few bad habits. It can't be that serious."

But it is that serious. A common misconception is that everyone is going to inherit the kingdom of God. These "little things" don't really matter that much. That simply isn't consistent with scripture or the teachings of the Church. We must take seriously the warning of St. Paul. How do we live our lives? What kind of choices are we continually making? Are we striving to live a life that produces fruit of the Spirit?

St. Paul presents a stark contrast in the details between the fruit of the flesh and Spirit. What I appreciate about his list is that it is so concrete and so obvious. If you are living according to the flesh this is what your life is going to look like. Done. That's it.

Now, I don't believe this is to say that it is all or nothing, that one lives totally according to the flesh or the Spirit. This is where the tension lies and where our spiritual growth is measured. Most of us probably produce mixed fruit, kind of like a fruit cocktail. But it is immensely important that we be honest with ourselves.

We need to admit that we produce fruit that is of the flesh. Take a few minutes to pray and reflect on that list. My guess is that a couple of the fruits may jump out at you. If you are not sure, take the bold step and ask someone else, someone who will be totally honest with you and ask them what they see. Don't just ask someone who is going to blow fairy dust at you. The fruits can be seen, so ask others what they see. Ask God to send his light and illuminate your heart. At times we may have a blind spot that we are not able to see. But it can't remain hidden all the time; other people see it and hopefully there is someone in your life who will care for you enough to point it out for you.

I want the fruit of my life to be of God. I want my fruit to be life-giving to everyone I encounter. If this is the type of life we want, at times it will require that God does some pruning so that only good fruit is produced. A good examination of conscience and confession often do the trick. Prayer is immensely helpful. Having people in our life (bible study, prayer group, and so forth) who are also seeking holiness with whom we can be accountable is such a blessing. It's a great gift to have brothers and sisters who love us enough to encourage us to live a life of virtue and at the same time remind us when we are not.

FRUIT OF THE SPIRIT

Years ago I was meeting with a zealous group of people who focused a great deal on the gifts of the Holy Spirit. I listened to them speak passionately about the need for the gifts and agreed with many of their points about how we need the gifts of the Holy Spirit. My struggle wasn't really related to what they said about the gifts; rather, it was that nothing was said about the fruits of the Spirit. And not only was nothing said about them, there seemed to be a lack of fruit. Now, before everyone goes all wild and accuses me of judging them, I share this story in order to express the frustration that was going on in my mind and heart. I was hearing so much said about the gifts but was becoming irritated and, honestly, somewhat disillusioned by what I was and wasn't seeing. Many of the people in the group, especially the leaders, were very harsh in their dealings with others. I did not experience patience, encouragement, and mercy from them but rather hardness and rigidity. Some of the leaders were often angry and spoke very negatively about people with whom they disagreed. Many in the group were convinced that their way of following the Lord was best and this had created factions and disunity in the larger community.

All this is to say that many of the people in the group sought with great passion the gifts of the Spirit (which again, I supported and believe is wonderful), but what frustrated me was the manner in which they went about it and how they related with others. The same people did not seem to be *producing* fruits of the Spirit. While it is a gross exaggeration, it was all gifts and little fruits, and I had a very difficult time with this approach. I believe that the proper use of the gifts should produce fruits of the Spirit. St. Paul makes this clear in 1 Corinthians 13 when he says he is nothing if he has the gifts of the spirit but not the fruit: love. The gifts should produce fruits in us.

St. Paul lists what these fruits are: love, joy, peace, patience, kindness, generosity, faithfulness, gentleness, and self-control (Gal 5:22–23). It should be noted that the *Catechism* lists twelve fruits, adding chastity, modesty, and goodness (CCC 1832). (The discrepancy lies in the translation of the original text from Hebrew and Aramaic to Latin. Modern translations have nine fruits while the older Vulgate translation has twelve.) The *Catechism* speaks of the fruit of the Spirit as "perfections" that the Holy Spirit performs in us. The fruits are signs or manifestations that our life is being transformed or perfected by God. As one is able to see fruits of living according the flesh, the same is true for the fruit of the Spirit. What then does this fruit look like?

Joy is a concrete sign or fruit that the Spirit of God is working in your life. St. John XXIII is often called the "happy pope"; he spoke of joy being a sure sign of the Holy Spirit. Pope Francis has said time and time again that Christians need to pray for greater joy. When speaking of joy in his apostolic exhortation *Joy of the Gospel* he says, "Joy adapts and changes, but it always endures" (7). In another place he humorously reminds Christians that we must not constantly look like we are returning from a funeral (10). As a fruit of the Spirit, joy is the lived awareness that God is faithful, loving, and merciful and that he will never leave us orphan.

For me, patience is the banana of the fruits of the Spirit. In my opinion, if a banana is not perfectly yellow and firm, it is spoiled. If there is even a spot of brown on it, I leave it for one of the other friars who likes them that way. Too brown and they are destined for the freezer to be made into bread. The point is, bananas have a shelf life of about eleven minutes before they spoil. It seems patience spoils quickly, too. Oh, to have a dollar for every time someone has asked me to pray for patience for them. Probably because our world is so busy, fast, and stressful, patience is often the first fruit to go bad. So often we get angry and blow up over the most insignificant things. A truly patient person is such a beau-tiful witness. If someone is patient, it is the first attribute used to describe them: "Oh, Kathy is the most patient person I know." This is probably the case because it's so rare. How would your daily life appear if you were more patient with your spouse, children, or colleagues? A lot more peaceful right?

Speaking of rare, how about self-control? When I reflect on most of the stupid things I have done in my life, some sinful and some just dumb, a great majority of them are because I lacked self-control. What an incredible power there is in a person who is able to control himself. Often when asked why I did this or that my answer was an enlightened, "I don't know." Well, I do know—I lack self-control. Think of all the daily activities that are impacted by self-control: eating, drinking, sleeping, speaking, exercising, and praying. This is a short list, but it reflects how integral the practice of self-control is to living a fruitful life.

And the greatest fruit is love. Love is the fruit that comes from my relationship with God. The more I experience what it means to be loved by God, the more I am able to love. I believe the spiritual life is a journey that leads me into a more profound experience of the love of God which purifies and transforms me. God's love changes me and shows me what it is to truly love. I look to Jesus and see how sacrificial love is and am more willing to lay down my life for others. I see how Jesus was motivated by love rather than merely obligation, and I am set free from the law. Hopefully over time our lives become so changed that we don't merely make mental choices to love (while that is good), rather, love becomes our natural way of dealing with people. We become so consumed by the spirit of God that love is our default. Oh happy day!

Imagine for a moment what this would look like. Imagine someone describing you based on the fruits of the Spirit. You are so generous, kind, gentle, and loving. Aren't these the qualities we want to be reflected in our lives? Isn't this the core of what you want your children to learn from you? I want people to look at me and see the attributes of Jesus, and when the fruits are more present in my life that is exactly what they will see.

Some of you may be thinking to yourself, "I just don't think that is realistic. I don't think it's possible." And you are correct: left to yourself, to your flesh, it isn't possible. That's the point, we aren't on our own, rather, we can be led by the Spirit of God and when we do this, our life produces great fruit. And other people notice this fruit.

Once when I was returning home from college for Christmas break I was on a flight from Pittsburgh to Phoenix. About an hour into the flight a guy locked himself in the bathroom of the plane. He then began to shout profanities and bang on the walls of the bathroom. The flight attendants tried to get him out of the bathroom, but he wouldn't come out. It was a stressful experience, and many of the passengers were anxious. The flight ended up having to be diverted to Chicago where we were met at the gate by two Chicago police officers. The officers came on board and forcibly removed the disruptive passenger. The woman next to me was frustrated by the inconvenience of the situation. Eventually, the flight once again departed for our final destination of Phoenix when everyone settled in for a time of uncomfortable napping. A couple of hours passed, and the pilot interrupted our restless resting. He informed us that due to the unscheduled stop in Chicago, we had used more fuel than expected. He explained that we were going to have to stop in Albuquerque in order to get more fuel so that we could reach our destination. Well, the woman next to me became apoplectic. "This is ridiculous. I can't believe this! I will never fly this airline again!" All the while I was considering our options. "Ah, come on Captain, let's give it a shot!" While it is always inconvenient to run out of gas while driving on the highway, I can only imagine the inconvenience of an airliner running out of gas. The woman looked at me with steam coming from her ears and blurted out, "How can you stay so calm!" Actually, I kind of felt she was frustrated and angry enough for the both of us. But what she was really saying was, "Tell me what animates your life, what allows you to stay calm and peaceful." It was such a clear example to me that others notice the fruit and the Spirit and desire to have this fruit in their life.

FRUIT PRODUCES MORE FRUIT

The fruits of the Spirit don't just stop with you and your life. There is a twofold blessing to the fruits of the Spirit. There is the blessing you receive as well as the blessing the fruit provides to others. When our life is producing fruit of the Spirit, we are more peaceful, calm, joyful, patient, and loving. All of this blesses us and those around us, making our lives more abundant. Just think about how your spouse would be blessed by you being more patient. I know, right? The fruits of the Spirit are to be tasted by everyone with whom we come in contact. Other people will be richly blessed if our lives produce good fruit.

Finally, and this is key: Most people I meet have absolutely no idea, and honestly probably don't care, that I pray every day. They don't know what specific gifts the Lord has given me. But they notice if I'm an impatient jerk. They can see whether or not I am generous, self-controlled, or loving. Everyone sees that. The whole world witnesses this and the world is blessed by fruits of the Spirit. Over time, other people are changed by such fruit. Your generosity invites others to be generous. Obviously not every act of generosity will be reciprocated, but over time it will have an impact. From here we begin to witness the hundred-fold. Seeds of the Spirit are planted in the hearts of people we meet every day. And over time, as they are nourished and watered, they begin to grow in the individual and fruit blossoms. By our lives of love we pollinate everyone we meet and this has the potential of producing an abundant harvest for the Lord. May our lives produce such a harvest.

Questions for Reflection

1. Being specific, what fruits, both good and bad, are most abundant in your life?

2. How would your life be different if you had more patience
    or any particular fruit of the Spirit?

Try this . . .

Take some time to pray asking God what fruit of the Spirit he
would like to develop in you. For the next month focus your
attention on growing in that one area.

5
THE SPIRIT BAPTIZES US

When is the last time someone asked if you have been baptized in the Holy Spirit? My guess is that few Catholics have actually been asked that question. I remember the first time someone asked me. I had decided to take a year off from college and spend it with a Catholic evangelistic ministry in St. Paul, Minnesota. As I arrived to the National Evangelization Team (NET) Center, my mom told me that the group was probably charismatic. I was vaguely familiar with the term but didn't know what it really meant. I asked what it was and she said something about the Holy Spirit. I was pretty serious about my faith and had prayed for the Holy Spirit before so I asked if I was charismatic. She stated that she thought I was but that the people with NET were probably going to be different from my experience. Boy was she right.

After I got settled into my room at the NET Center one of the people on staff informed me that there was going to be a "prayer meeting" later in the evening and that I was welcome to attend. I thought a little peace and quiet after a long day would be great so I said I would be there. It all started off okay until the first song was over after which everyone kept on singing and hollering and carrying on. Some of the people were waving their hands in the air and praying out loud. Every now and then I could make out what they were saying, but sometimes it sounded like gibberish. (I now understand they were praying in tongues.) I found myself frustrated wondering how God could ever hear me over the commotion. I remember having an anxious feeling; their prayer was so different from my usual experience. However, in an odd sort of way I was intrigued by what was happening. There was something very, well, alive about the way they prayed. It was odd; I was both attracted and put off by what was taking place.

The next day Steve, a fellow Netter (that's what you call a person who is with NET), walked up to me and asked if I had been baptized in the Holy Spirit. I thought it an odd question. I told him that I was baptized as a baby like everyone else.

"No, no not that, *baptism in the Holy Spirit*."

"I don't really know what you are talking about so I guess I haven't."

"Well, then we need to lay hands on you and pray over you."

I doubt it!

Apparently, a very common way for individuals to experience this "baptism in the Holy Spirit" was to have someone pray with them and this often involved laying on of hands. Well, I kindly thanked Steve and told him that I would get back to him when I wanted him to "lay hands on me" but that if he felt so inclined that he should feel free to start praying without me.

BAPTISM IN THE HOLY SPIRIT

Baptism in the Holy Spirit? What is it? Even though I was an active Catholic, I had never heard the term. Heck, in seventh grade I won the local catechism bee but never had that question. I asked one of the other Netters who appeared to be pretty normal but also seemed to know what was going with the whole baptism in the Holy Spirit thing. She said that it was really just being "filled with the Holy Spirit." She told me that I could read more about in the scriptures. That sounded like a pretty good place to start to me.

I began reading the scripture and found that being baptized in the Holy Spirit (or words similar) is mentioned in each of the gospels as well as the Acts of the Apostles. (See Matthew 3:11; Mark 1:8; Luke 3:16; John 1:33; Acts 1:5.) John the Baptist made it clear that he baptized in water but that Jesus would baptize in the Holy Spirit. It became apparent to me that what I experienced as a baby might be different than baptism in the Holy Spirit.

In his gospel, Luke said that we would be baptized in the Holy Spirit and in fire. Again in the Acts of the Apostles, Luke has Jesus instructing the apostles to go back to Jerusalem and wait for the "promise of the Father" and the "baptism of the Holy Spirit" (Acts 1:5). When I read the various accounts of the baptism in the Holy Spirit I didn't necessarily have a better understanding of exactly *what* baptism in the Holy Spirit was, but I was able to see that it was important. It seemed to be something that Jesus intended for us, and it changed people.

The scripture states clearly that Jesus came to baptize us in the Holy Spirit. It seemed to me that if this is one of the reasons Christ came, then perhaps I was missing something. As I made my way through scripture, I was also able to see *the effects* of the baptism with the Holy Spirit. From my reading the Acts of the Apostles it appeared to me that the disciples experienced the baptism in the Holy Spirit at Pentecost. It became clear that the baptism of the Holy Spirit enabled the apostles to do something that they were unable to do before. Before Pentecost they were locked in a room paralyzed by fear and after experiencing the Holy Spirit they boldly proclaimed Jesus. Something changed in them.

Slowly, I was beginning to see more clearly what the baptism in the Holy Spirit might be about. It seemed to be about power. The disciples' experience of the Holy Spirit gave them the power to escape the confines of a locked room where they were bound by fear. It gave them the power to witness to Jesus' resurrection and the ability to faithfully live the Christian life.

A few days passed with me asking lots of questions and staying away from Steve who still had the goal of "laying hands on me." This idea was still bugging me.

FILLED WITH THE SPIRIT OF GOD

I had been with NET for several days when I found myself spending the evening in the small chapel at the NET Center. It was a typical chapel of a Catholic Youth Center, and by that I mean circa-1970s yellow shag carpet, lots of large pillows, and few chairs. The chapel had the painting of Jesus that I fondly refer to as "surfer Jesus." You know the one where Jesus has flowing locks, sculpted beard and mustache, eyes searing your soul. The altar was simple, in the front and center with a small tabernacle off to the right. The red glow of the sanctuary light was providing all the light in the chapel.

The chapel was not particularly beautiful, but it was unbelievably peaceful.

It was late and there was only one other person in the chapel off in the left corner. I was sitting against the wall in the back right corner, and I remember having an honest conversation with God. I shared with him that I was confused and really didn't understand everything that was going on. I had all kinds of questions running through my mind. But, in the midst of the confusion and all the questions, I remember feeling safe. I had a deep sense of God's presence and even with so many questions, I was calm.

My prayer that night can best be described as an emptying of my mind and soul. I was pouring my heart out to God, laying all my questions and concerns before him. At one point I prayed, "God, I don't understand this baptism in the Holy Spirit or charismatic thing, but if you want this for me then I want it." At that moment I experienced the presence of God in an unbelievably tangible, powerful way that forever changed my life.

I would never be the same. It wasn't simply a cool experience or a merely powerful event. It was a life-changing encounter. The Holy Spirit came upon me and I could feel something overshadow me. It was both exhilarating and a little scary. I had never experienced before what I was experiencing. I didn't totally understand what was going on but the best way to describe it is that I was being filled; I was being filled with the Spirit of God.

Or was it a release? Yes, maybe that was it, something was being released. It's kind of hard to describe really. But what I do know is my life has never been the same since that moment. As the Holy Spirit welled up in me I began to quietly pray and quickly the Holy Spirit began to pray through me. I began to pray in tongues, even though I didn't ask for it. (Is that legal?) Suddenly, Romans 8:26 made sense to me. ("The spirit too comes to the aid of our weakness; for we do not know how to pray as we ought, but the Spirit intercedes with inexpressible groanings.") I knew I was no longer in charge and God was directing me. I experienced what I now understand to be the baptism of the Holy Spirit. The Lord met me where I was and blessed my life.

INNOVATION AND INHABITATION

It's neither my desire nor my expertise to present a thorough historical account or a deeply theological discussion on the experience of baptism in the Holy Spirit. This has been done by others far more qualified than I am. However, there are a few points I would like to briefly explore that might be helpful.

I recall leading a retreat for a wonderful group in North Carolina. We were talking about the Holy Spirit, the gifts, and the baptism in the Holy Spirit. One of the participants blurted out, "Why have I never heard of this?" On another occasion I was having lunch with a very active Catholic involved in various ministries. We were talking about the Holy Spirit when he stated, "I've been Catholic all my life. Why haven't I ever heard any of this? Why is the Holy Spirit a stranger?"

Questions and reactions such as these are pretty common. I wish I could give an answer but I really don't know. Not that it all depends on priests, but I don't know why the Holy Spirit isn't preached on more. While in seminary I don't recall ever speaking about the baptism in the Holy Spirit. All I know is that it would be helpful if we as a Church talked about the Holy Spirit more. There are lots of Catholics like the ones just mentioned, who are active and hungry but have never heard about these things. There are also Catholics who are kind of stuck in a rut and desperately, like all of us, need more of God's Spirit.

How is it possible for someone to be baptized, confirmed, and attend liturgy but seemingly not live a vibrant life of faith? And yet, either by personal experience or by observation, we know that this is not only possible but fairly common. Lack of faith, connection to the world, evil, or lack of understanding could be part of the reason. Fr. Francis Sullivan, S.J., would look to St. Thomas Aquinas and explain that the individual needs to experience a "new sending" of the Holy Spirit to release or unlock the grace already present in the individual.

This experience of a sending of the Holy Spirit can be understood to be the baptism in the Holy Spirit. Aquinas would posit that when a person experiences this sending of the Holy Spirit, the individual may experiences a type of "inhabitation or indwelling" of the Spirit. The individual may experience a presence of God as if something from outside rests upon them. This is the presence of God's Spirit and it speaks to my experience and resonates with what happened to me many years ago in the small NET chapel. This explanation also resonates with many people I have met and prayed with over the years.

Sullivan goes on to detail how Aquinas stresses that when an individual has experiences such as this, a type of "innovation" results. New things begin to happen in the person. It may be a new love for prayer or scripture, seeing Christ in the sacraments, or a desire to share one's faith or a newfound power over sin.[1]

While I have never been married, the days and weeks following my experience at the NET center were *honeymoonish*. Perhaps first and most importantly, I experienced Jesus as being alive in my heart and life. He was not merely a wonderfully loving, forgiving, wise Son of God who once walked the face of the earth, but he was alive and was animating my life. I was encountering the resurrected Jesus. Growing up I never really questioned God's existence, but perhaps I simply took it for granted. But after this experience there could be no doubting or taking this reality for granted. God was real and he was alive. Everywhere I looked I saw God. He showed me his love, truth, mercy, his light and presence. I saw God much more for who he was rather than who I had made him out to be. The supernatural power of God came alive for me. In my experience of the baptism in the Holy Spirit, or a new sending of the Spirit, I felt as if I was bathed in a river of grace. Rather than water being poured over me, God's grace showered me and anointed me. I began an amazing journey that continues to this day.

FOR EVERYONE

I was visiting with a bishop in Tanzania, Africa, and he shared with me that he would not ordain a man to be a priest if he had not experienced the baptism in the Holy Spirit. "How can I ask or expect him to do the work of Jesus if he does not have the power of Jesus?" he explained. And yet, we try to live the Christian life on our own power and giftedness, only to fall again and again. We need help. We need the active presence of the Holy Spirit in our life. I believe that each and every Catholic Christian needs to experience the outpouring of the Holy Spirit. We all ought to pray for our own Pentecost experience, the baptism in the Holy Spirit, the promise of the Father, what we call it is not as important as what we experience when we encounter the Holy Spirit.

My experience tells me that there are a lot of people like me who have lots of questions and sometimes fears about the Holy Spirit. You may think of past experiences or people you know who have had "Holy Spirit experiences" and they cause you to be uncomfortable. Maybe you don't believe you have a "charismatic" spirituality. My concern is that because of this uncomfortableness we inhibit the workings of God's Holy Spirit. We don't experience the transforming grace that he desires for us. We don't experience the full power of God (or more of his power; do any of us really feel his full power?), and we often live our spiritual life in a locked room. I don't believe it is God's will that we live the Christian life locked in a room and without the Holy Spirit to free us, but this is where we often live.

One of the greatest gifts for me from this experience was a power in my life that I did not previously have. In Romans, St. Paul is frustrated because he does things he doesn't want to do and doesn't do things he wants to do (Rom 7:15). This was my life story. The baptism in the Holy Spirit gave me great power to be the person God wanted me to be. Not that I never fail, but I have much more victory than I did before.

The grace of baptism in the Holy Spirit is not something for only a few. Nor is it an experience relegated to people involved in this or that movement. It is a grace for the Church; a grace for all the People of God. In a remarkable address on Pentecost 2008, Pope Benedict stated: "Today I would like to extend this invitation to everyone: Let us rediscover, dear brothers and sisters, the beauty of being baptized in the Holy Spirit; let us be aware again of our Baptism and of our Confirmation, sources of grace that are always present. Let us ask the Virgin Mary to obtain a renewed Pentecost for the Church again today, a Pentecost that will spread in everyone the joy of living and witnessing to the Gospel" (May 11, 2008).

And most recently Pope Francis stated, "I hope you will share with all in the Church, the baptism in the Holy Spirt."[2]

I think it's important that we recognize that Pope Benedict called us to "rediscover" being baptized in the Holy Spirit. I think that many in the Church have lost, have forgotten, or most likely, have never known about this grace. That must change. It's imperative that we each experience the presence of God's Holy Spirit, which gives meaning to our very existence. This is not something we only experience once but something that we can continually experience. Here lies a danger of the term "baptism in the Holy Spirit" in that it makes it sound like it is a one-time deal. On the contrary, God wants to continually send his Spirit to us.

Another risk is to look for specific gifts or charisms in order to determine whether or not someone has experienced this grace. The thinking goes that you need to have a particular gift in order to show you have experienced baptism in the Holy Spirit. I don't believe this would be accurate. There isn't a specific gift that is a "proof" of having experienced this grace.

This experience is going to look different depending on the individual; God meets us where we are. But I think it is fair to say that a person who experiences baptism in the Holy Spirit will experience a deeper love of the Lord and their faith. They will experience more profound conversion and see more fruits of the Spirit. They will receive greater power to live and witness to their faith.

I believe it is vital that we experience the blessing of the Holy Spirit that unlocks God's grace. My prayer is that everyone is able to go before the Father and with honesty and sincerity say to God, "Send your Holy Spirit to me, fill me with your Holy Spirit, and baptize me in your Holy Spirit." If this is something you have done, then do it again. If you are like me, you have prayed this prayer many, many times. Do it one more time. I believe this prayer represents what should be our consistent stance before God. We don't just pray it once and then move on. Rather, we continually go before the Father and ask for his Spirit. Pope Francis exhorts us, "do not forget to frequently invoke the Holy Spirit, every day . . . it is important to pray to the Holy Spirit."[3] This ought to be the Christian's stance before our loving God.

Finally, lest I forget, a few days after my experience of the Holy Spirit when I was on NET, I ran into Steve. "I guess I am open to having you 'lay hands on me' and pray for the baptism in the Holy Spirit." I still didn't fully comprehend all that had happened. He informed me that I had experienced it. "I am not sure when, but you already experienced it. You are different, I can tell." And he was right; I was different.

Questions for Reflection

1. Is your faith life lived more "out there" or in a locked room?
2. What has been your personal experience of Pentecost?

Try This . . .

Very simply take a few minutes and pray that God would baptize you in the Holy Spirit and fire.

6
THE SPIRIT IS UNLIMITED TO US

We are all aware of men and women who have served in the military and have had to live on food rations. There are also the poor who by necessity must live on rations. It's never been my experience.

I suppose the closest to rations I have come would be times when I would go camping. On one particular camping trip, my father, a couple of friars, and I went to the Upper Boundary Waters on the border of Minnesota and Canada for a five-day trip. We rented canoes and paddled and portaged from lake to lake. We had to carry everything we needed for the five-day expedition so we spent a lot of time thinking about what would be necessary for our trip. Before we started the trek we were concerned about the weight of our backpacks. We would have to carry tents, sleeping bags, rain gear, fishing gear, and of course, food. The thought of trusting in the Lord, taking very little food, and relying on caught fish to feed us briefly crossed our minds, but the words of Jesus "do not put the Lord your God to the test" rang loudly in our ears.

Plus, we had never fished for walleye and pretty much didn't have a clue what we were doing.

We meticulously considered what we would need for each breakfast, lunch, and dinner as well as snacks. We then went through a cost and weight analysis. Now, the cost was not a financial cost but rather the cost related to the weight and size of a particular food item. Some foods are light but take a lot of room in the backpacks while others are heavy and just not practical. Puffed wheat, while a great breakfast food and very light, takes up too much room and is pretty awful without milk (more weight). The thought of a couple of beers while fishing was very attractive; the reality of having to carry them was not. No beer. No puffed wheat. This wasn't going to be easy.

After a protracted discussion, we finally settled on a menu, packed everything we needed, and were ready to go. We loaded our backpacks and canoes onto a van and began the twenty-minute ride that would lead us to the lake where we would begin our journey. Arriving at the lake, I was somewhat disappointed and surprised that we went through half of our allotted snacks for the week on the short van ride. At least the bratwurst made it. I began to wonder if perhaps we didn't pack enough food. Let the rationing begin!

The first day was the longest and most difficult. We canoed and portaged through what seemed to be half of Minnesota's ten thousand lakes but was probably closer to ten. OK, maybe five. After about six or seven hours of canoeing and portaging we settled on a campsite and began to set up. After a really long day we were all exhausted and extremely hungry. We unpacked the food and were surprised; at the grocery store it looked like a lot more food. In the middle of the wilderness it looked like a scant supply. Looking at the food, we were all thinking the same thing: "There is no way that is going to be enough food."

We sized each other up with a very troubling "I'll do what I have to do to stay fed" look. At that moment I was thrilled that I was not the largest. Suddenly, I wished I had taken more seriously all those useless survival role-playing games I was forced to do in various team-building seminars. We assured each other that we would be fine. If we stuck to the menu and did not deviate, there would be no problem. And let's not forget that we would certainly catch some fish. We continued to set up camp, and I secretly began hoarding granola bars.

We had a certain amount of food, and each day we used what was available to us. While we knew there was more food, we also knew that we could not eat it. Obviously, the food was limited, so rationing made sure that we would have enough to last the entire trip. In the end, we ended up making it out of the Boundary Waters without starving due to a little luck fishing and a bit of rationing.

As limited human beings, we are constantly rationing. We ration time. Everyone has one thousand, four hundred, and forty minutes in a day: no more, no less. While it seemed Mrs. McGregor's math class itself was one thousand, four hundred, and forty minutes long, it wasn't the case. One thousand, four hundred, and forty minutes. That's it. And each of us rations our time. We determine who or what is going to get some of those precious minutes. If we give too many minutes to one project, we won't have enough for something else. We try to save time and not waste it.

We ration our energy. We make decisions about what we will and won't do depending on how much energy it will take from us. We have all said at one time or another, "I just don't have the energy for that now."

We ration money.

We ration ourselves. There is only so much of you to go around. We live and breathe in a limited world and as such we must ration.

God is not like that.

He does not ration his Spirit.

MORE THAN ENOUGH

While the grains of sand in the world's deserts and the stars in the heavens are measured in numbers so huge that they are beyond comprehension, they are still limited. There are a certain number of grains and stars.

God's Spirit is without limit. His Spirit is not rationed; there is always more. The heart of Jesus is a floodgate for his Spirit for which each of us possesses the key to release that Spirit. All we need is to ask in faith, and the Spirit will be released. The waters of the Lord's Spirit never run dry, and God never has to hold back his Spirit just in case someone else may be in need.

John's gospel states this clearly. "For the one whom God sent speaks the words of God. He does not ration his gift of the Spirit" (3:34). God always wants to make his Spirit available to us in whatever situation we may need. God is eternal, and as such, his Spirit is an eternal wellspring. Never once has he been left empty; the well never runs dry.

Take a moment and prayerfully reflect on this reality. God does not ration his Spirit. Jesus is not in the heavens eyeing a gauge as he releases his Spirit. "Hmmm, how much should I give Coleen? I should probably hold on to a bit just in case Kevin needs some, too." It simply does not work like that. The heavenly Father never chides his Son, "Hey there, not so much, save some for others."

There is an interesting story in 2 Kings. It is the story of the prophet Elijah and his disciple Elisha. Somewhat confusing, I know; they are two different prophets with similar names. Elijah and Jack would have been so much easier to remember. At any rate, it is clear that Elijah is near the end of his ministry and Elisha has a request of him. "May I have a double portion of your spirit?" (2

Kgs 2:9). Much has been written about this "double portion" that Elisha requested, and it is interesting to note that Elisha is responsible for twice as many miracles as Elijah, but the underlying point is that while Elisha's request was an extravagant "double portion," it nonetheless was limited. Elisha requests a double portion, and Elijah grants him a double portion of his spirit, which is wonderful and generous. But it is still a portion.

In one sense this is actually somewhat difficult for us to grasp since we are limited and finite. Everything in our world is rationed, is limited. God's grace isn't. An ocean of God's spirit is a beautiful image, but still limited. God in his infiniteness shares his infinite Spirit with us.

Perhaps because we think there is a limited supply, we don't ask God often enough to send us his Spirit. Perhaps this is one of our fundamental struggles: it's not that we ask for too much of the Spirit; rather, we don't ask enough. God desires to give more of his Spirit, and we need to become more comfortable in asking for this. I ask for more of the Holy Spirit a lot. I always carry a small single decade rosary with me. If I am not using this to pray the Rosary, I often use it to ask for more of the Holy Spirit. With each bead of the rosary I simply say, "Come Holy Spirit." Over and over again I pray "Come Holy Spirit." It's so simple, but it has been a great blessing in my life. It is an easy reminder of my need to be filled. Long ago I made a deal with the Lord that this action, the moving from bead to bead, would be a prayer for more of the Holy Spirit. I knew there would be times when I would be required to focus on something else that would not allow me to think about my prayer, but I could still move the beads through my fingers. There are times when this is habitual, but my prayer remains the same. As my thumb moves from bead to bead, my prayer is for more of God. Each time I do this it is a simple request that God would share his Spirit with me.

EXPAND OUR HEART

On a number of occasions, I have had a similar image when asking God to send his Holy Spirit. The image is of a heart. In the image our heart is kind of like a balloon. The first time you blow up a balloon it takes a bit of effort. Obviously, as you are blowing, the balloon is being stretched as it fills with air. If you were to let the air out of the balloon, it would look different, kind of shriveled. Now, if you were to attempt to blow the balloon up a second time, it would be easier to do given that the balloon has been stretched. However, were you to continue to blow up the balloon and make it bigger than the first time, it would once again become more difficult.

I think this is kind of how we work with the Lord. We allow our hearts to be filled by God but only to a certain point. We ask him to fill our hearts and he does. However, we don't think about the fact that perhaps our hearts may leak. Over time, maybe from lack of attention, maybe from sin, our hearts slowly deflate and are in need of being filled again. We ask God to fill us, and being a faithful God, he does. But we only allow it to a certain point and oftentimes not to where we are stretched. God wants to give more of his Spirit to us, to expand our souls, to bless us with more of his grace, his gifts, and more of his very life. Sadly, we often don't ask for this. Maybe we don't know that there is more available to us so we just don't ask. Or maybe we have asked in the past and God hasn't come through in a way that *we* wanted or expected, so we don't bother asking again. The bottom line is that I think God wants us to ask for more of his presence. Recall once again Luke 11:13 where Jesus invites us to ask for the Holy Spirit. Don't stop asking.

This is so important because what we need more than anything else is God. This may sound odd or even harsh, but more than we need prayers answered, more than we need healing, we need God's

Spirit. This is just so foundational and fundamental to our faith. If we have a deeper relationship with the Spirit of Jesus, allowing his spirit to animate our life, then this affects everything else. We will look at everything and respond to everything differently. Imagine for one month, if multiple times a day you would stop whatever you are doing, take a deep breath, and pray three times: "Come Holy Spirit." That's it. No long, complicated, or prolonged prayer—just, "Come Holy Spirit." If you were to do that ten times in one day, it would take roughly one minute. I imagine God will bless this prayer. He delights in sending his Spirit to us.

JOY OF THE SPIRIT

God desires us to have the joy of his Spirit moving on us. The more open we are to his Spirit, the more we will experience this. And when the Spirit moves, we experience a God of surprises. We often think of the Lord when we are in need. "Help" is the most common prayer. But God wants to be more than a lifeguard at the beach. God can show himself to us in many other ways and circumstances.

St. John XXIII said joy is the surest sign of the Holy Spirit's presence. I think an authentic joy is one of the most attractive Christian attributes. We all gravitate toward people who exhibit joy. In a homily, Pope Francis stated that "a healthy Christian is a joyful Christian. . . . Joy is the seal of a Christian. Even in pain, tribulation. Even in persecution."[1]

This is probably why Pope Francis titled his apostolic exhortation *Evangelii Gaudium* (The Joy of the Gospel). In this letter, the Holy Father uses some type of the word "joy" more than one hundred times. He has also on several occasions stated that many Christians have the face of a "pickled pepper; sour-face, or sour-puss." I suppose we can debate the translation of these words and phrases, but there is no confusion in the meaning: Christians must radiate joy.

There's something really beautiful about unbridled joy. I remember as a kid the joy I experienced spending an afternoon on a river with my family. Being there with my mom and dad, sister, and four brothers was always such a wonderful time. What elation there was as a little boy every time I, or anyone, caught a fish. We all rejoiced when we heard those three magical words: "I GOT ONE!" My joy and excitement wasn't something I had to manufacture; it was an authentic, spontaneous celebration

Or the simple joy when your favorite team wins the big game. When I was growing up, my two favorite NFL teams were the Denver Broncos and the Minnesota Vikings. Until 1998, that had me at zero and eight in the Superbowl. Good thing I didn't like the Buffalo Bills or that may have been more than my little heart could stand. The Broncos beating the Packers for their—*my*—first Superbowl was a joyous occasion. To this day I think I may have scared one of the elderly friars as I jumped up on to my chair in a fit of joy.

And the joy of the Lord is even greater than that.

Joy was standing before the congregation moments after having the bishop lay hands on my head ordaining me to the priesthood. Tears of joy running down my cheeks, as well as my mom's, dad's, sister's, brother's . . . You get the point. God was present.

What a blessing it has been for me to be invited to preside at many weddings. I love looking at the face of the groom as his bride walks down the aisle. Pure, holy joy.

Surely one would expect joy, expect God's presence at such events. But the depth with which one can experience this joy is only possible through grace. But it is also the times when you wouldn't necessarily expect it where God often surprises us. One occasion that was a total surprise was when I was able to take my teenage niece and nephew to a performance of *The Lion King* on Broadway in New York City. It sounds cheesy I know, but there's no way I can explain the joy I experienced when looking at the faces of my niece and nephew. There was something beautifully innocent in their faces. They were enthralled with the performance. Their eyes were bright, as children's eyes should be, and at that moment they didn't have a care in the world. But for me, that moment was graced. I experienced the presence of God in a profound way. I can't really explain it, but there was a Spirit of joy that was so real, so rich and deep that I knew in the depth of my soul that God was present. I began to simply pray, and I thanked him for a moment that was blessed. I believe that experiences such as these can be more common if we continue to seek the Spirit's presence in our daily lives. This same event with my niece and nephew could have been a fun time, a memorable time, but perhaps not the graced moment that it was.

Perhaps the ultimate surprise of the Holy Spirit that brought abundant joy would be the annunciation of the coming of Jesus to the Virgin Mary. St. John Paul II pointed this out at a General Audience when he was speaking about joy and the Holy Spirit. "The Gospel is an invitation to joy and an experience of true and profound joy. At the annunciation, Mary was invited: 'Rejoice, full of grace' (Lk 1:28). Mary's joy is realized with the coming of the Holy Spirit, who was announced to Mary as the reason for rejoicing" (June 19, 1991).

One may ask, "How can Mary not rejoice? She is going to be the mother of God!" To which one may respond, "How can she not rejoice? Really? How about being pregnant, unwed, a virgin, carrying the Son of God, and facing harsh punishment by the religious leaders? Oh yes, and all of this revealed by an angel. Other than that?"

Mary was invited by Gabriel to rejoice and rejoice she did. In the midst of all of the questions, all the difficulties previously mentioned, and even fear, Mary—full of the Spirit—ultimately

responds with her graced Magnificat: "My soul proclaims the greatness of the Lord and my spirit rejoices in God my savior" (Lk 1:47).

As is always the case, we learn from Mary. She rejoices because
she has been overshadowed by the Holy Spirit. God's will is
unfolding in her life, and Mary rejoices in this. The circumstances
don't matter that much because she knows that God is present.
The world will want her to focus on the problems and obstacles,
to look at all the potential negatives—and there are many—but
Mary rejoices.

And Mary is not the only one to be filled with the Holy Spirit
and joy. Elizabeth proclaims that when Mary spoke she was filled
with the Holy Spirit and "at the moment the sound of your greeting reached my ears, the infant in my womb leaped for joy" (Lk
1:44). What a great image of John the Baptist leaping for joy in
his mother's womb! How I would love to see a sonogram of that.
What must Elizabeth felt having her child leap with joy?

It seems to be such a natural response. We are filled with the
Holy Spirit, and we respond with joy. St. Paul points out that this
is central to the kingdom of God. He states to the Romans that
"the kingdom of God is not a matter of food and drink . . ." (I have
to chuckle given that this is often the scripture for evening prayer
on Thanksgiving Day) ". . . but of righteousness, peace, and joy in
the Holy Spirit" (14:17).

I believe there is such a need for this particular grace at this
precise time. There is so much stress in the world today and everyone is so serious and burdened. Pope Francis was prophetic in
writing about the joy of the Gospel. If we come to know the love
of God and the saving grace of Christ, we must respond in joy. If
we continue to be filled with the unbridled, unlimited presence
of God's Holy Spirit, then joy must be our natural and reason-
able response. We would then sing with the angels our traditional
Christmas hymn:

> Joy to the world! The Lord is come
> Let earth receive her king!
> Let every heart prepare him room . . .

Questions for Reflection

1. Mary was "overshadowed" by the Holy Spirit. What does her encounter with the Holy Spirit reveal to you about God?

2. How would your spiritual life be different if you didn't ration yourself with God but gave all you had to him?

Try This . . .

First, pray that the Holy Spirit would use you to bring joy to another person's life. Second, in the next three days bring joy to another person's life. Be concrete.

7

THE SPIRIT ADOPTS US

Oftentimes we limit the Holy Spirit to being a type of personal assistant. That's not totally bad. I mean, I count on the Holy Spirit to help me with a lot of very practical things. More times than I care to remember, I've asked the Holy Spirit to remind me of someone's name. Sometimes the Spirit comes through; sometimes I'm left hanging. Of course there was the time I introduced myself to a student and she said her name was Mary Elizabeth. I shared that it would be easy for me to remember her name given that she had the same name as my sister. She smiled and responded, "That's what you said the last time we met." Exactly.

Very often when we need something we call upon the Holy Spirit and expect the Spirit to perform. Remarkably, the Spirit often does work this way; we should never stop calling on the Holy Spirit and seeking the Spirit's assistance. However, the Spirit wants to do so much more than be a type of spiritual app for our smart phone. The Holy Spirit doesn't merely want to help us out a bit or make us a little more patient; rather, the Holy Spirit wants to move in a way that changes how we see our very selves, how we see God, and how we relate to him.

St. Paul lived under the absolute conviction what when Christ and his Spirit break into our lives, we can and should be radically different (2 Cor 5:17). Christ has rescued us from a life of sin and has broken the bonds of death. Through Baptism and the Holy Spirit, we have been raised up so that we are no longer slaves, but we are a new creation. We are God's children. As God's children we are no longer led by a spirit of bondage or slavery, but we are led by God. Paul writes, "For those who are led by the Spirit of God are children of God. For you did not receive a spirit of slavery to fall back into fear, but you received a spirit of adoption, through which we cry, 'Abba, Father'" (Rom 8:15).

Because we have been saved by Christ, we are not slaves and should not live as if we were. Reflect on the relationship of a slave and master. Very simply, a master owns a home, land, animals, and slaves. It is a relationship rooted in fear, control, obedience, and obligation. The slave is always in fear of upsetting the master, never wanting to do anything that would make him mad for dread of punishment. The slave is always looking for scraps from the master's table. The slave constantly strives to make the master happy by performing as the master wishes. A slave does not approach his master freely; rather, he cautiously approaches, waiting to see his master's mood. If the master is happy with the slave, good things may come to the slave and his family. Paul states emphatically that we have not received that type of spirit.

How do we know if we have a spirit of slavery? Try reflecting on the words you might use to describe your relationship with God. Be absolutely honest because this is between you and God. What words would you use? If you only or predominantly use words like fear, shame, obedience, punish, or distant, it may be that the Lord wants to free you from a spirit of slavery.

Ask yourself:

- Do you approach God mostly out of fear?
- Do you feel like you need to do lots of good things in order to earn God's love and blessing?
- Do you try to appease God?
- Is God on your side, or do you have more of an adversarial or confrontational relationship?
- Do you feel God is watching you, waiting for you to mess up?
- Are you a slave or a child?
- Is God your "master" or your loving Father?

GOD'S ADOPTED

Depending on how you answer most of these questions, you may be trapped by a spirit of slavery. You were not created to be a slave and God hasn't chosen you to be his slave. You see, we are God's children: his sons and daughters. This is a fundamentally different relationship than that of a slave. No, we have not received a spirit of slavery but a spirit of adoption which causes us to cry out "Abba" or "Daddy."

The Father loves each of us and makes us his own. He bestows on us the title of son or daughter with all the rights, privileges, and blessings that go with being the kid of a King. We are God's adopted, and he is our Father.

But why adopted? Why does Paul say to the Romans that we have received a spirit of adoption? Is it better to be adopted? There must be something unique and special about Paul choosing that word. Most of us don't really know what it is like to be adopted or to adopt.

A good friend of mine adopted a child from Haiti and shared with me his experience. He reflected that before the adoption he wondered what it would be like to receive the child.

"How would I connect with him? How will we bond?"

He then went on to tell me that the very first time he saw the child, through a thick glass window in the airport in Miami, that he felt, he knew, "That child is my son!"

He went on to share how his heart was filled with an intense fatherly love—a love that wanted to protect, a love that was full of joy. There was an immediate understanding that this little boy that he had seen for the first time would forever be his son. He explained that this child that he had previously only seen in pictures had filled his heart with a tremendous love. He didn't have to manufacture, decide, or will to love his new son; it simply poured from his heart.

There is something profoundly beautiful here. Something striking about being God's adopted. Adoptive parents make a choice to adopt a child, perhaps choosing one among many. We want *this* child, and they bring the child into their home. The child will forever be a part of the family. In a strange way, my parents never did that for me. I was conceived out of their love for one another, and well, they've been stuck with me ever since.

It was not like that in Roman law, however. A parent could actually disown their own birth child. If they did not like the sex of the child, the way the child looked, or if the child had a deformity, the parent could disown the child. However, this is not the case with adoption. When a parent adopted a child, they knew exactly what they were getting—the good and bad. When a parent adopted a child, it was permanent; the child could never be disowned.

God is like this with us. He knows everything about us, the good and the bad, our strengths and our brokenness, and he still chooses to take us into his family. St. Paul stresses this with the image of the spirit of adoption which makes us God's children. He states this again when writing to the Galatians, "As proof that you are children, God sent the spirit of his Son into our hearts, crying out, 'Abba, Father!'" (4:6).

DADDY GOD

Once when I was a pilgrim in the Holy Land, I went on a walk with a fellow pilgrim through the Muslim quarter of Jerusalem. We stopped by a few of the shops in the area, and while we were in one of the small gift shops, we struck up a conversation with the owner, who was Muslim. He was interested in where we were from, and we enjoyed a rather lengthy conversation with him. We talked about his family and what it was like to live in Jerusalem. Given that we were pilgrims, we spoke of our faith. He was very courteous and listened respectively. He even asked us questions about our faith. It was an extremely interesting and wonderful conversation.

As it turned out, we were once again in the area later in the week, and the owner of the shop saw us and called out to us. Once again we struck up a wonderful conversation that lasted probably fifteen or twenty minutes. This conversation was different though. As if we had developed some level of trust, the focus of our conversation was faith. At the time I knew very little about the Muslim faith and asked all kinds of questions. I don't know how many conversations he had had with a Catholic priest, and he seemed to enjoy asking me questions as well. We agreed on lots of points, but in one sentence, things changed. I don't recall exactly what led to it, but I spoke of God as a loving father and of me being his child. "No, no, God is not Father. We would never dare speak of God as Father. God has many, many names—Father is not one!" He was quite adamant and seemed offended by what I had said. I explained that I believe God is my Father and shared that Jesus had called God "Father" or *Abba*. I went on to explain that as a son, I am able to have an intimate relationship with my Father God. To which he responded, "No, this is not possible."

This encounter shed light for me on why some people were so frustrated and angry with Jesus. Rarely in the Old Testament is God referred to as a "Father," and never is he referred to as *Abba*. So when Jesus spoke of God as *Abba*, it was groundbreaking. No one ever before had addressed God with such a title.

They certainly would have used titles such as Almighty, Lord, God Most High, and so forth. All of these make sense.

But *Abba*? Daddy? Never would religious leaders of Jesus' time speak of God in that manner. I struggle trying to find something analogous for us to understand how shocking this was to the ears of Jesus' listeners. The faithful Jew would understand an otherworldliness to God, a God who is mighty and powerful. However, in one word uttered by Jesus, the very understanding of God would change.

Abba. Jesus refers to God as *Abba*.

God is a loving Father and when the Spirit is poured out on us, we cry out, "*Abba*." His spirit does not move us to cry out "Yahweh" or "Mighty God." Instead, we cry out as Jesus did: "*Abba*."

The Spirit then draws us into a relationship, a triune relationship. The Spirit of Jesus beckons us into his relationship with his Father, and the Spirit, and through grace, reveals to us that Jesus' Father is also our Father. We don't come to that reality on our own, but the Spirit leads us to God, and when our hearts see him, we instinctively cry out *Abba*. We have a Father.

Every child wants and needs a father. I was incredibly blessed to have a very wonderful father. My dad loved God, loved my mother, and loved me. In that order. What more could I ask for? Well, as a little boy I wanted him to also be at my baseball games. As a Little League player, my games were on weekday mornings during the summer. My dad would often take an hour off of work and come to the park and watch my brothers and me play baseball. He wasn't able to watch the entire game, and some days he couldn't make it at all, but I always knew he would try and was certain that he wanted to be there. I realize it may seem like a little thing, but to a little boy, it was a big deal. My dad was there for me.

But that is not everyone's story. I know lots of people who never really knew their fathers. Some of these people lived in the same households with their fathers and never really felt loved, wanted, or protected. There is an emptiness in their hearts that needs to be filled. We all long for the love of a father. Sadly, many people look to fill this emptiness with things that will never satisfy. I remember sharing with a young man that we have a father in heaven who loves us very much. He looked at me with tears in his eyes and went on to explain that his father had left his family when his parents divorced. He explained that he was able to see his dad on a regular basis but that he wished his dad would never have left. "Why did he leave us? Why did he have to leave me and my brothers?" I could not answer him but told him that God would never leave him. I explained that God is a Father who will always be there for him and will never walk away. In John's gospel, Jesus promises us that we will not be orphans (Jn 14:18), and Psalm 27:10 tells us that even if our father and mother leave us, God will always take us in. Upon hearing this, the young man wept.

As a Father, God is our provider. He gives us everything we need in order to be faithful to him and live a life full of his love and joy. This does not mean that God will give us everything we want. I think most fathers are aware that they can't, won't, or shouldn't give their children everything they want. But surely, they will do their best to give their kids everything they need. God never fails us in providing what we need most.

God is a patient father. He wants each of us to come to him, and he patiently waits for us—he gives us time to repent and return to him (2 Pt 3:9). This is so amazing; while we wander away from God in search of our own paths, God patiently waits for us to return. He's always waiting for us. One of my favorite scriptures on this topic is Luke 15:17–18:

> Coming to his senses he thought, "How many of my father's hired workers have more than enough food to eat, but here am I, dying from hunger. I shall get up and go to my father and I shall say to him, 'Father, I have sinned against heaven and against you. I no longer deserve to be called your son; treat me as you would treat one of your hired workers.'"

What I love about this excerpt is how the son "comes to his senses" and returns to the Father. That should be all of our stories. We've probably all wandered away from God to one degree or another. However, in a moment of grace we come to our senses and return to our Father who deeply loves us. And as we all know, the Father patiently waits looking for us so that he may run to us and welcome us home.

God our Father also disciplines. The author of Proverbs encourages us not to despise the Lord's discipline (Prv 3:11). And the author of Hebrews writes, "My son, do not disdain the discipline of the Lord or lose heart when reproved by him; for whom the Lord loves, he disciplines" (12:5). Discipline should always be connected to love. My parents disciplined me because I was their son and they loved me. When my friends and I did something wrong, which you can imagine was extremely rare, my parents only disciplined me, not my friends. It was not their place to discipline others. They disciplined me because I was their son and they loved me. They had a sense of obligation that I should be disciplined when the situation warranted.

Discipline without love could be merely punishment or humiliation, and this is not how God deals with us. When we are disciplined it is not God getting back at us or punishing us because we have sinned or done something wrong. One of the ways I experience God's discipline is a type of sadness. It's as if I've disappointed my loving and kind father, and this causes me to feel sad. The Father uses this to correct me, to point me in the right direction, to bring me back to him. The Father loves us, and as such, he will discipline us because he wants what is best for us. Discipline should teach and instruct, and if doled out properly, it can even encourage.

Sometimes the discipline we receive may merely be the result of the choices we make. If we cheat in school or steal something from work and get caught, there will be consequences. God can use these consequences to teach us, to allow us to be disciplined.

Finally, and often this is hard to understand and accept, God also uses life's trials, our crosses, to discipline us. Some of these crosses are allowed by God while others are sent. All of them exist in order to bring us closer to God. He is not mean or harsh. Rather, God is a faithful Father, and he always wants our best and will do whatever needs to be done, in love, to bring this about. This is apparent in a story that a father shared with me as his daughter was struggling with a severe illness: "Obviously, I wish my daughter wasn't sick, but God has been so close to me. Through my little girl's sickness my wife and I have had to rely more on God. In the midst of our difficulties God has shown himself to us. I know more now what it means to trust in God."

THE GOLDEN CHILD

I am sure that Aga and Lazar had it difficult. I mean, can you imagine being the sibling of Mother Teresa? "If only you were more like your sister." If you think that would have been difficult, can you imagine if Jesus would have had birth brothers? Tell me that wouldn't have been rough. "Well, your brother brought Lazarus back from the dead this morning, and you are still in bed. If you are not going to work miracles, could you at least clean your room?"

Jesus was the perfect son. That doesn't mean he didn't make mistakes—maybe he spilled his milk or broke Mary's favorite vase—but he never sinned. Jesus is the perfect son, and his Father is the perfect father. Jesus, as a son, can teach us what it means to be a child.

More often than I can remember people have shared with me that their father did this or that wrong. No father is perfect, and I think maturation includes realizing that our parents were not perfect—none are. However, on far fewer occasions have people said to me, "I wasn't a very good son/daughter." Sure, it has happened a few times, but compared to complaints against parents, it's no contest.

The Spirit moves in us and reveals God as *Abba*. God is our Father and we are his sons and daughters. And with that being said, I think I could be a better son. We could all probably be more faithful sons and daughters. I want to be a more obedient son and listen more carefully to what the Father asks of me. I am sure we could be more helpful children. There are always people around us in need, and the Father depends on us to reach out to them, to offer them help and assistance. So often, we are selfish and only concerned about our own wants, needs, and desires. Jesus was always reaching out to those in need, and we could probably do more to help others.

One more thing: I could be a more grateful son. God has been so good to us, and we could definitely thank him more. We could give more back to him, be more generous. A fruit of the Holy Spirit is gratitude, and we ought to show this more for a God who is so good.

Finally, I am sure the Father would like to spend more time with each of us. It's good that our heavenly Father is not petty because, if we are honest, we mostly come to him because we want something. I think that would get tiring, but it doesn't seem to for God. In fact, we are *encouraged* to take our requests to the Father. However, at times it may be good to simply go to the Father in order to spend time with him. No real agenda—just make ourselves present to him as he desires to be present to us.

INHERIT A KINGDOM

Our God is Father and our Father is King. That's makes us heirs of a kingdom.

Pope Francis put it this way:

> The Spirit itself, together with our spirit, attests that we are children of God. . . . And if we are children, we are also heirs of God, joint-heirs with Christ. . . . This is the precious gift that the Holy Spirit places in our hearts: the very life of God, life as true sons, a relationship of confidence, freedom, and trust in the love and mercy of God. . . . Let us allow ourselves to be guided by the Holy Spirit, let us allow him to speak to our hearts and tell us this: that God is love, that he is waiting for us, that God is the Father, he loves us as a true Father [Papà].[1]

This means that as children, we have all the rights and privileges accorded to us as heirs. These rights are not something that we earned, but they were earned for us by another son, Jesus. His death and resurrection, our Baptism, and subsequent choice to live for Christ afford us the same benefits Jesus had as the son of the Father. We are able to approach God as a son or a daughter would, not as a slave—not out of fear, but out of love. We can approach God and speak to him, not because of our holiness or goodness, but because we are his children.

As his sons and daughters, we are to inherit the kingdom of God. Sadly, many don't make their claim against the estate. Can you imagine being told that you are set to inherit ten million dollars and not claim it? Ridiculous, right? But for many Christians, they don't claim the inheritance that Christ has won for them. The offer is always there (it is irrevocable), but all too often many don't respond. All we need to do is say yes. We say yes to the lordship of God's son, Jesus. Yes, we want to live as God's son or daughter. Yes, we want to stop living for ourselves and start living for him. That's it. We may fall every now and then, but as long as we keep getting up, we will reign forever with our Father who rules in heaven.

Questions for Reflection

1. What stirs in your heart when you hear that you are God's adopted, he has personally chosen you, and that he wants to be in a relationship with you as your Father?

2. How do you experience being a child of God?

Try This . . .

Get away for a few minutes and be still. Ask the Spirit to show you ways that your image of God is not correct. Ask the Spirit to show you the Father.

8

THE SPIRIT MAKES US HOLY

It's a problem when you need a new king. I mean where does one look for a king? Angie's List? Personals?

I recall being in Greece and a guide was telling us how the country needed a new king so they went looking. Representatives of Greece spoke to various royal families in Europe informing them that they were looking for a king. She stated that they were having a hard time because, "We didn't have much money and aren't very obedient." Ya, I could see where that may be a problem.

The Lord also needed a new king, and the Spirit led Samuel to search for this king. (See 1 Sm 16:1–13.) Samuel was instructed by the Lord to go to Bethlehem where the Lord had identified one who would be king. Jesse had eight sons to choose from so Samuel believed that surely the Lord's anointed was present. However, God reminded him that God does not see like man sees, rather he looks at the heart. In a wonderful scene Jesse begins to present his sons to Samuel one by one.

"Nope not this one, not him, nor him . . ."

One has to think that by the fourth or the fifth son, Jesse may have been getting a little frustrated. I mean, these were his boys of which I am sure he, like any dad, was very proud.

Four, five six, seven . . . none of them. Not one!

"The Lord hasn't chosen any of these; you don't happen to have a few more do you?"

As a matter of fact, Jesse does have one more, the youngest. But given that he is the youngest, he has pulled the short straw, as the youngest *always* does. David is tending the sheep. Samuel wants to see David the youngest, most insignificant son.

I wonder what the conversation was like when they called for David.

"Um, David, a prophet named Samuel is here and the word is that one of your father's sons is to be anointed king. Well, at the moment we are zero for seven so he wants to see you."

"A king? Us? Anointed? Really, why me?"

"Well, that's exactly what we thought."

"What about Abidadad? He's the oldest and brightest."

"I know, right? But the prophet says no."

"Well, surely Shammah! He's charming, communicates well, and people love him. He would make a great king."

"That's what I thought. But, no, not him or any of your brothers. Samuel wants to see you. He said something about not seeing as man sees, but God sees the heart."

As David approaches, the Lord says to Samuel, "There—anoint him, for this is the one" (1 Sm 16:12). In front of David's brothers, perhaps to the surprise of everyone, Samuel pours oil over David. The oil flows from the crown of his head, off his youthful face, dripping from his chin and running down his chest. "Anoint him. . . . God does not see as man sees." Samuel anointed David and the Spirit of the Lord rushed on him. (See 1 Sm 6:7–13.)

THE SPIRIT RUSHED

The Lord chose David and as oil covered him, the Spirit anointed him and rushed on him. What a great image: the Spirit rushing on David. I can't say exactly what this may have looked like, but I think I may have some kind of idea what it may have felt like. I have experienced that rushing of the Spirit and pray you have as well. It ought not be limited only to David. The Spirit ardently desires to rush on all of God's people.

On many occasions when praying for the Holy Spirit I have felt the Spirit's rush. My experience at the NET Center was a life-changing experience of the Spirit rushing upon me. But there have been many other times that may not have been as dramatic but still extremely significant. I've experienced this rushing when alone praying in my room or when preaching during Mass. I experienced it during the Litany of Saints when lying prostrate before the altar on my ordination day and while driving in the car praying for a family member who was ill. The movement of the Spirit is not quarantined to a particular place or time but seeks out hearts willing to receive.

What then does it mean to say that the Spirit rushed? Often times it is difficult to use words to explain religious experiences or truths about God. Perhaps this is why Jesus often used every-day stories or examples to explain such things. "Do not hide your lamp under a basket" (Mt 5:15) or "the kingdom of God is like a mustard seed" (Mt 13:31). With that in mind, I'll give this a shot. The rushing of the Spirit is similar to a breeze that one walks into. Imagine walking in a city and turning the corner around a building to feel a breeze rush against your face. You become aware that the building was shielding the breeze, but once out of its protection you become aware of the gust. It's sort of like that.

Or recall walking into a department store on a cold day, and as you enter the store from the outside there is a warm flow of air that you walk through as you enter the store. It's kind of like that, but not totally.

Maybe one more. Have you ever seen the process of a donut being glazed at a Krispy Kreme donut shop? If not, you must. Sending a man to the moon and fresh hot glazed donuts are definitive signs of the progress of humanity. The fresh-cooked donut comes out of the hot shortening and is moved to a conveyer belt that will eventually end at the glazing station. The plain donut inches its way to a hot lava flow of glazed goodness, which each donut slowly passes under. The donut is covered in a warm glaziness. Yes, the Spirit rushing is sort of like that.

The Spirit flows over us and covers us. It may not be something we necessarily *feel* from our external senses, but we feel it in our spirits, our souls.

This "rushing" can happen any time. There are moments when I experience it and it is totally unexpected, while at other times it is when I am asking for the Lord's presence. One such occasion was when I was on a flight to Africa. This flight took place a few months after the September 11 attacks, and I was flying to Tanzania where, about a year prior, the United States embassy had been bombed. I fly a lot and rarely have any anxiety about flying, but this flight was different. It was about three hours into the flight and for some reason, I suppose the events of September 11, an unreasonable fear came upon me. I can't honestly say what the object of my fear was—perhaps it was the plane crashing, an act of terrorism, or something else, but I was filled with anxiety and was sweating as if I had played racquetball for an hour. I felt paralyzed with fear. I can't recall ever experiencing anything like this before or since. I sat in my seat holding on to the armrests and tried to calm myself. I tried to take deep breaths and remind myself that everything was going to be fine and nothing was going to happen. All to no avail. I don't recall how long I was in this state; it seemed like hours but was probably more like many minutes. Eventually, I cried out, "Jesus help! Send your Spirit to calm my frightened heart." At that moment I felt as is if my body was standing under a hot shower (or warm glaze if that analogy works for you). Beginning from my head to my toes, I felt the Spirit rush over me. In that moment the fear and anxiety were overcome by the Spirit of God. It was a remarkably stark, concrete, and immediate experience of the presence of God. There was no doubt in my mind that the Spirit made himself present to me at that moment and brought me his peace.

I think God wants to come to us like that more often. I believe if we were to call upon God's Spirit more habitually, we would have more encounters of God and experience his grace and power more regularly.

YOU'RE CHOSEN

God has chosen each of us and wants to send, his Spirit to us (Jn 15:16). However, many people actually question this. Maybe on one level some individuals get it, but it goes something like, "God has chosen me? Sure, God has chosen everyone."

But, it is a lot more than that. God always works in the personal. He hasn't just chosen everyone, Christ has chosen you; he's chosen to send his Spirit to you. The personal choosing is a little harder to grasp, but it is really important that we do. God has chosen you personally and desires to bless you with his Spirit.

At times, we may wonder why God would do this, and this is a consistent theme in the scriptures. Moses wondered why him, particularly because he did not speak well (Ex 4:10–13). Jeremiah thought someone else may do a better job (Jer 1:4–10). And the scribes and Pharisees questioned Jesus' choice of friends and followers (Mk 2:16).

I have heard and said so many similar things.

"Why me? I feel so inadequate. There is so much I don't know. There are other people who are holy, and I can see why you would choose them. But me? Do you know what I've done? (OK, a silly question.) God are you really choosing me? Me out of all the others?"

I've also heard, "Why him or her! They don't have a clue what they are doing. They may look holy to everyone else, but I know them. I know what they are really like. Jesus, are you sure that's the type of person with which you want to be associated?" (Another silly question.)

The choosing of David provides us with really beautiful images that give light to the movement of God's Spirit and his choosing us. First, we are reminded that it is God who does the choosing: "You did not choose me, it was I who chose you" (Jn 15:16). For reasons that we may not totally understand, God has chosen us— you and I—first and foremost to be in relationship with him. David did not go looking to be chosen; God came to him and the Spirit rushed on him. God saw something in David that others were not able to see. We so often get caught up in external appearances: what someone looks like, how they perform, how smart they are, or where they come from. God doesn't seem to be influenced by those things. Rather, he sees the heart. And in David God saw "a man after God's heart" (Acts 13:22).

The Lord saw David and chose him. First, and most importantly, God saw that David's heart was turned toward God. This is key. David had turned his heart to God, he loved God and desired to be faithful to him. That said, David was not always faithful; at times he failed miserably. It is fundamental that we understand this. God saw David and knew all that David was going to do, and God still chose him. God still chose David even though he would take Uriah's wife, Bathsheba, as his own and have relations with her that would conceive a child. David would attempt cover up his sin by trying to arrange that Uriah and Bathsheba could have relations so that he could claim the child was not his. When this did not work, David plotted to have Uriah killed in battle (2 Sm 11:1–6). And God still chose David.

God knew David. I don't believe David surprised God and in Psalm 139 he, David, reflects on this:

> Lord, you have probed me, you know me . . . you understand my thoughts from afar . . . Where can I go from your spirit? From your presence, where can I flee? . . . You formed my inmost being; you knit me in my mother's womb. I praise you, because I am wonderfully made . . . My very self you know . . . When I was being made in secret, fashioned in the depths of the earth.

God knew David better than David knew himself. I think God knew that David was weak and that he would fall. But God also knew that David had turned his heart to God. And while he would sin in dramatic fashion, he would also repent in similar fashion (2 Sm 12:13–16). With all of his flaws and his weakness, God still chose David and sent his Spirit on him.

I believe this is also true with you and me. God didn't choose me thinking that I would be a perfect priest without sin. Hardly. He chose me because he wants to anoint me and be in relationship with me. He chose me because, responding to his grace, my heart is turned toward him. He is my center, my focal point, my true north; he is my Lord. At times I may get distracted and turn away, but with his grace and his pull, I am able to turn back. The wonderful part is that God continues to choose me and he chooses to send his Spirit upon me so that I may continue to turn back toward him. His Spirit rushes on me and invites me to be filled by his grace.

God has chosen you. He invites you to turn your heart toward him. God knows how you are beautifully and wonderfully made, because that is how he made you. He knows that at times you will die to yourself for the good of others. Jesus knows how you go out of your way to serve and help those in need. God knows that sometimes you bite your tongue and don't say what you may be thinking.

He also knows that you will fail, that at times you will turn your heart only toward yourself or any number of other things that will lead you away from him. God is fully aware that at times you won't bite your tongue. Christ still chooses you and wants to send you his Spirit in order to draw you into a more intimate relationship with him. God has chosen you and me for a purpose. God has chosen us to be holy.

BE HOLY

The spirit of God makes us holy (2 Thes 2:13).

What do you imagine holiness to look like?

I think many people have a stereotype of what it means to be holy. The image is often of someone else and more often than not someone strikingly similar to an English butler: stuffy, very serious, and not much fun. Holiness is generally reserved for priests and nuns (hence, not much fun) and even to only a select few of them. For those who are holy, we may respect them and be inspired by them but not really able to relate to them. They are different from us.

I think it is fair to say that many people are either not interested in being really holy or approach the idea with great caution. There is a negative perception about being holy and at times it is used in a pejorative light.

"Oh, she is holier than thou!"

"They think they are *so* holy."

What does that mean? An informal poll regarding a life of holiness produced descriptions like serious, prayerful, saintly, and disciplined. Of course all of those are good. But rarely is there a mention of joy, freedom, attractive, or desirable. Perhaps this is why many people don't take seriously enough the invitation of God to allow his Spirit to make them holy.

In the end, holiness says more about God than it says about us. Holiness is about God working in our lives and our cooperation with this work. One can't become holy simply by a decision and hard work. One can become a better pianist by dedication, focus, and working hard. Or one can become a better tennis player. But holiness does not *simply* come about by a decision. To be clear, it does involve a decision. We have to make a personal decision that we want to be holy. From that point, it is our willing it and surrendering to God's spirit that allows this transformation to happen. However, we are destined to a life of frustration if we think we can become holy by merely willing it through our own strength and power.

From the time I was making adult decisions about my faith, I wanted to be holy. For the longest time my prayer was very simple: "Make me holy." My desire to be holy is one of the main reasons I became a Franciscan and a priest. I remember when I was in my first year of formation in my Franciscan community. This first year is called postulancy, and a postulant is probably slightly lower than a plebe, cadet, or even a freshman. There's not much lower than a postulant. Even a novice is higher than a postulant. As a postulant you look up to those who are "in vows." Your goal is to one day be where they are: the green pastures of vowed life.

One day during a time of recreation I was feeling particularly celebratory. A friar who had already professed vows said to me, "Dave, I used to think you were holy, but now I realize you are an extrovert."

Hmmm.

I see.

OK, then.

I joke about this, but at the time it was somewhat of a vocation crisis. I reasoned that if I was going to be holy and a Franciscan friar, then I should probably be quieter. I should probably not joke around. I shouldn't short-sheet the novices' beds. I figured that I ought to bow a lot more and perhaps carry incense with me at all times. I was quite certain that really holy priests must always have incense. One never knows when a little incense may come in handy. I would later learn that my personality type is a rarity in religious life. Most religious are introverts and are pretty ordered; I am a strong extrovert and am not always the most ordered person and am sometimes too spontaneous. Seminary training is often difficult for people like me. "Why spend so much time reading about ministry? Let's just go do it!" I recall fondly one of my professors writing me a note at the end of my time in seminary thanking me for sticking with it.

Over time and after many meetings with both my spiritual director and formation directors, I came to realize that the friar's statement was simply foolish. For me to be holy is for me to be the person that God created me to be. The entire event identified the problem that many have. The perception is that holiness is the Trappist monk—not the rambunctious postulant, or busy CEO, or auto executive, or stay-at-home mom. This must change. God calls each and every baptized Christian to be holy and sends his Spirit to us so that we may be holy. It is a blessing to look to the saints as models, but sometimes this perpetuates the problem. We need more models of saints who were busy moms and dads, business men and women, and married people. Chapter five of *Lumen Gentium* states that every Christian is called to a life of holiness. It should be a part of the Christian's DNA. Also, article eleven of the same document states that spouses in Christian marriage "help each other to attain holiness." I always tell newly married couples that they get to make each other holy.

John 17:18 reminds us that we have been sent into the world and this is where we live a life of holiness. We can't build a wall around us hiding us from the world. After St. Francis converted, he stood on the peak of a mountain looking at the Umbrian Valley and stated, "The world will be my cloister." Everyone's cloister is different. For some of you, your cloister is your minivan littered with crushed Goldfish crackers and melted gummy snacks stuck on the backseat upholstery. For others, it will be the office cubicle surrounded with people who try to draw all life out of you. Wherever your cloister is, God wants to bless you and give you all the necessary grace in order to make you holy. While you may often feel that the only way for you to be holy is by escaping your situation, the reality is that God's Spirit can meet you where you are and fill you with his grace. No matter your situation or circumstances, God is there.

A life of holiness is going to look different for each of us, but there will be some elements that I imagine will be present in each person. First, a total commitment and surrender to the person of Jesus. The Christian is no longer living for one's self but lives for God. St. Paul put it this way: "I have been crucified with Christ; yet I live, no longer I, but Christ lives in me; insofar as I now live in the flesh, I live by faith in the Son of God who has loved me and given himself up for me" (Gal 2:20). Conformity with Christ is an undeniable mark of a man or woman being made holy. They strive to love as Christ loved and forgive as he did. Their lives image that of Jesus.

Holiness causes men and women to live their life animated by the Spirit of God. This empowers them to be faithful to the Gospel and Church. Their faithfulness is marked by joy rather than dread or solely obligation. The fruits of the Holy Spirit are readily visible in men and women who are seeking radical holiness.

Holiness is a life marked by conversion and charity. The individual is not perfect, but she is striving for perfection and seeking God's mercy when she falls. Life is just as difficult and complicated for one who is holy, except that God's presence brings him comfort and peace.

God has created each of us to be holy, and it is God's desire to anoint us and make us holy. It really isn't about how smart we are, how wise, talented, or good-looking. It's not even because of our goodness or strength—it's about the Lord and his ability, through his Spirit, to make us holy.

Christ has chosen each of us to follow him. He has sent his Holy Spirit to us so that we may respond to this call which will draw us into a life of intimacy and holiness with Jesus our Savior.

Questions for Reflection

1. God sees and knows everything about you and still chooses you; he wants to be in relationship with you. Thoughts?

2. If others were to look at you and describe you as being holy how would that make you feel? Why?

Try This . . .

Turn your heart to God. Perhaps you have done this a million times, but take a few minutes, ask the Holy Spirit to show where you heart may be divided, and turn once again to Jesus.

9
THE SPIRIT BRINGS US FREEDOM

"Freedom Tastes like Guacamole." This phrase on a billboard caught my eye as I was driving along the expressway outside of Pittsburgh. Freedom is one of my favorite topics so when, out of the corner of my eye, I saw in huge letters "freedom," I had to take another look. In the background on the billboard was a huge bowl of guacamole along with a couple of avocados, onions, and bright red tomatoes for a little color.

Freedom tastes like guacamole? OK, I love guacamole as much as the next guy, but come on, guacamole—freedom? That's ridiculous.

I love freedom and pay attention to how freedom is spoken of and how it is marketed. Yes, sad but true, freedom is marketed. What can only be described as a potential trademark issue, one need only do a very brief search and see other claims about the taste of freedom. Apparently it ranges from wine, beer, bourbon, candy, diets, frosting, gum, coffee, orange juice, ice cream, cigarettes (both tobacco and electronic), bachelor parties (last taste of freedom), and motorcycles. There is a credit card available named "Freedom." Credit cards selling freedom? *Come on, man!*

As Americans we are inundated with images and illusions of freedom. Part of this is clearly because, as Americans, we see freedom as a core principle to our way of life. Deeper still is that, as human persons, there is something innate in us that knows we were created to be free. While we may appreciate the role of government to help protect freedom, our freedom doesn't ultimately come from government—it comes from God. God alone is the source of authentic freedom, which is simply defined as living a right relationship with God.

The human person was created to be free, and it has always been that way. In the beginning God created us in freedom, but that freedom was lost due to our sin and disobedience. Freedom was restored by Jesus' life, death, and resurrection. St. John tells us that "when the Son sets you free you are free indeed" (Jn 8:36). St. Paul reminds us of this in Galatians: "For freedom Christ has set you free" (5:1).

St. Paul also tells us that wherever the Holy Spirit is, there is freedom (2 Cor 3:17). If we are going to be radically free, the Holy Spirit is going to play a significant part in leading us to freedom. However, we must first deal with why it is that we are not free.

LOSE THE WEIGHT

I remember hearing a story about a young man who sarcastically asked a preacher, who had just preached on the weight of sin, about what the weight of sin really means.

"I don't feel the weight of sin. How heavy is it? Ten, twenty, fifty pounds?"

The preacher waited a moment and asked, "If you laid a five-hundred-pound rock on a corpse of a person who had died, would the person feel anything?"

"Don't be silly. The person is dead, he's not going to feel anything," the young man retorted.

"The person who doesn't know Christ is also dead and isn't able to know the weight of their sin," responded the preacher.

We can't be free from something that binds us if we are not aware that we are bound. Sin is very much like that. We are all bound by sin and are often totally unaware of this. We go through our daily lives and are not aware of the sin that clings to us (Heb 12:1). I suppose on one level most of us know that we are sinners. We've been taught this since we were young. But do we really know the weight of our sin? Do we know specific sin? If we are going to confession, is it always the same thing? Are we getting to the root of our struggle? If we don't become more aware of these things then we continue to live in and be bound by our sin. This is not what Jesus desires for us; rather, Christ has freed us from the power of sin (Rom 8:2).

I think too often we go about trying to figure out our sin in the wrong way. Perhaps before confession we take a few minutes and try to just *think* about what we have done wrong. Now, this clearly is a good practice, but my guess is that it generally produces the same results. We take the burden of figuring out our sin upon ourselves. It's not necessary to do this alone; the Spirit of God is very happy to help us come to see our sin.

When someone comes to me for confession, I generally begin with a prayer that goes something like:

"Come with your Holy Spirit that Martin may know his sin, not to judge or condemn himself but so that he may know your mercy."

It's also worth pointing out how I end the confession. The prayer of absolution that the priest prays at the end of the confession points to the role of the Holy Spirit and forgiveness of sin. It's possible that you've never listened closely to what is said given that your job is done. But the priest prays, "God the Father of mercies, through the death and resurrection of your son, our Lord Jesus Christ, you have reconciled the world to yourself and sent the Holy Spirit among us for the forgiveness of sins."

The Holy Spirit is able to show us our sin. Oftentimes we just try to think about what we have or haven't done; we try to "figure it out" rather than asking for God's help. The Holy Spirit is our helper, even helping us know how we fail. In John's gospel Jesus says that he must go so that he can send his Holy Spirit to us. He then says that the Spirit will convict us of our sin (Jn 16:8). I think this is really important for us to grasp. Jesus sent his Holy Spirit to help us see our sin. To be clear, this is a blessing, a witness to God's love for us. The Holy Spirit is not some kind of spy working on Jesus' behalf. Rather, the Spirit showing us our sin is a sign of how much God loves us and will do everything possible in order to reveal that love. God loves us so much that he helps us see how we fall.

The Holy Spirit convicting us of our sin never leads to self-condemnation but always to the mercy of Jesus. If you are hearing whispers in your heart that are saying how terrible you are and how God could never love you or forgive you because of the things you have done, this is *not* the Spirit convicting you; rather, it is the evil one or the flesh. The conviction of the Holy Spirit leads us to the loving embrace of our Father. The Holy Spirit convicts to convert, not condemn. Feelings of unworthiness don't come from the Spirit, and it's important that we realize this. Again, in John's gospel (14:26) Jesus speaks of the Holy Spirit as being our advocate, not our opponent or adversary. It is the evil one who is our "adversary," which in Hebrew is "Satan." The movement of the Spirit always leads us closer to Jesus—never away from him.

On several occasions in my life I have gone through a time of pretty serious repentance. By that I mean I had a deep sense of my sin, but also a more profound understanding of what Jesus did in order to save me from my sin. On one occasion the text from the prophet Isaiah impacted me in a way that changed my relationship with the Lord, by allowing me to have a clearly understand of what Jesus has done for me.

> Who would believe what we have heard?
> To whom has the arm of the LORD been revealed?
> He grew up like a sapling before him, like a shoot from the parched earth;
> He had no majestic bearing to catch our eye, no beauty to draw us to him.
> He was spurned and avoided by men, a man of suffering, knowing pain . . .
> Yet it was our pain that he bore, our sufferings he endured
> . . .
> But he was pierced for our sins, crushed for our iniquity.
> He bore the punishment that makes us whole, by his wounds we were healed.
> We had all gone astray like sheep, all following our own way . . .
> Like a lamb led to slaughter or a sheep silent before shearers, he did not open his mouth.
> Seized and condemned, he was taken away . . .
> He was given a grave among the wicked, a burial place with evildoers,
> Though he had done no wrong, nor was deceit found in his mouth . . .
> Because he surrendered himself to death, was counted among the transgressors,
> Bore the sins of many, and interceded for the transgressors.
> (Isaiah 53:1–12)

Such beautiful and powerful words. Allow them to sear your soul.

My seasons of repentance have always been connected with the Lord inviting me to a deeper conversion. It seems as if maybe there is some kind of collaboration going on, that when Christ invites me to a deeper conversion, the Holy Spirit brings me to a deeper repentance. But of course this makes sense. As I grow closer to the light, I am going to be able to see my darkness more. Perhaps this is what John the Baptist was alluding to when he said that he baptized in water and repentance but that Jesus was going to baptize us in the Holy Spirit and fire. The Holy Spirit is fire and light, allowing us to see things to which we were previously blind. Fire also is used to purify, which the Lords does as we repent.

If we are going to be free, it's important that we allow the Spirit to do the work that Jesus charged the Spirit to do. We ought to pray and ask God for this grace. Let us pray that the Spirit would be a holy fire that would consume us. A fire that convicts us of our sin and help us to get to the root of why we continue to commit the same sin. Let's give God permission to burn away whatever is in our heart, mind, or soul that keeps us away from him and prohibits us from loving as we ought. We pray that we could come to know the sweet repentance that leads to the heart of God.

THE DESERT

Where the Spirit of the Lord is, you will find freedom; therefore, I want to be where the Spirit of the Lord is. That means that we need to go wherever the Spirit leads, and sometimes, the Spirit will lead us to the desert. This can't surprise us.

"Filled with the Holy Spirit, Jesus returned from the Jordan and was led by the Spirit into the desert for forty days, to be tempted by the devil" (Lk 4:1–2). St. Mark puts it a little differently; he states that the Spirit "drove" Jesus to the desert (Mk 1:12). Why he didn't just walk we'll never know, but it is clear that the Spirit led Jesus to the desert. As we allow the Spirit to lead us more, it's best that we prepare for our own wilderness adventure.

Before Jesus goes to the desert there is one last thing for him to do. In a show of solidarity with us as sinners, Jesus submits to John's baptism of repentance. Not because Jesus ever sinned and needed this but because we did. There in the middle of the Jordan River, the Holy Spirit rests on Jesus and anoints him for his ministry. Then the Father declares his pleasure in his Son Jesus. Jesus was not ready for the desert until he was "filled with the Holy Spirit" and had received the Father's blessing (Lk 4:1). Now he is ready and the Spirit says go.

Jesus going to the desert was a significant image for the people. The desert was a place where the Jewish people had spent a great deal of time. It was a place of wandering and searching, a place of temptation, and a place where the people had often failed miserably. It's as if the Spirit leads Jesus to the desert in order to make things right. The Spirit leads Jesus to the desert because men and women before him had experienced the desert and those who would come after him would also be led there. Jesus was going to show them and us how to survive in the desert. He would make the desert a sacred place rather than a barren wasteland.

What does Jesus' time in the desert teach us? First, and it's essential we get this, the Spirit led Jesus there. This needs to be the lens through which we view everything else. The Spirit of God was leading Jesus to the desert and sustaining him while he was there. For many, the desert represents that arid, dry, dangerous, painful place that we think is void of God. Whatever your view of the desert, it is a place where eventually every Christian will be led.

Sometimes we struggle with this, but it is a reality from which no Christian is able to escape. Deserts, wilderness, dryness, crosses, difficulties are all a part of our pilgrimage of faith—part of our life in the Spirit. At the heart of so many people's struggle is this basic issue. "Why the desert?" We so often fight to get out of the desert that we fail to recognize that God is present there. Jesus was led to the desert by the Spirit; he was not abandoned to the desert by the Spirit.

I am often asked why this or that is happening. I have to honestly reply that I don't know why specific things happen when and how they do. Oftentimes this is not what people want to hear but it is honest. I don't know why you are going through such a dry time. I'm not sure why God seems so distant to you right now. I don't know why your daughter was tragically killed in an automobile accident. I wish I could tell you why your marriage failed. I simply don't know. What I do know is that God is present. If you take nothing else, take this: God is in the wilderness with you. Keep in mind that beautiful Advent theme *Come Emmanuel*, which of course means *God is with us* (Mt 1:23).

This is what I hold onto most when I'm in the desert. God is with me; his Spirit will sustain me. The Spirit led me there and will help me. I also remind myself that it is not the Spirit that is doing the tempting. God does not tempt us; he is on our side. ("No one experiencing temptation should say, 'I am being tempted by God;' for God is not subject to temptation to evil, and he himself tempts no one" [Jas 1:13]).

Also, remember that the desert is a season. I don't know if it will be ten, twenty, or forty days, weeks, months, or years, but I know that it will come to an end. I will admit, that while in the desert this is not a great deal of consolation, it is true and I know the value of holding on to what is true.

I'm also aware that it is in the desert that my faith will be strengthened. Temptations make me stronger, not weaker. Temptations are just that, temptations. They are not sins, and they don't mean that I have fallen. The *Catechism* relates Jesus' time of temptations to Adam and Eve who fell when they were tempted by the serpent (CCC 528). Jesus is once again seen as fixing what went wrong in the past. We who come after Jesus are the beneficiaries of this; we may be tempted but we don't have to fall.

When we are in relationship with the Spirit we can overcome temptations. The Spirit helps us see more clearly exactly what's happening. If you are like me, I often travel too far down the road of temptation before I even realize what's going on. I find myself saying after that fact, "You should have seen that coming." There are circumstances and people that I struggle with and the Spirit is able to help me recognize the temptations before it's too late.

Also, things are not always what they seem. People often feel the reason they fall is because they are weak. The rationale is if only they were stronger they would not fall. I think that can be a subtle deception of the evil one. A common reason people fall is because they are discouraged, frightened, angry, doubting, or lonely. Weakness may not be the cause, rather something else. Jesus was hungry (not weak) and the Satan tempted him with food; he will do the same to us. If in moments of temptation we can ask the Holy Spirit to help us see what's going on, (you're lonely) we have a greater chance of overcoming the temptation without falling. The moment we recognize what is happening, we have a choice to make. Jesus *always* chose his Father; I make this same choice occasionally. I know that the Lord is faithful and he will strengthen me and guard me from the evil one (2 Thes 3:3), but sometimes I fail.

Finally, my history tells me that the times I fail the most are the times that I am not really serious about seeking God's help. For one reason or another (some of which have just been mentioned) I don't really want God's help and I go at it alone. This never ends well. What I have come to realize is that in the past I focused on a particular sin that I committed but I failed to see what may have led to that sin. It's possible that the first sin may have been not seeking the Lord's help and from there a myriad of things can go wrong. The Holy Spirit helps us to both see and overcome.

DESERT OR TEMPLE

Jesus' following the Spirit to the desert and his faithfulness there reclaimed the desert. What was before a wasteland becomes a place of victory and freedom. The Spirit makes holy the desert. One of the graces of the Spirit is allowing us to see God in places where we may not have noticed him before. Perhaps this is most powerful when we see him in our own lives.

"Do you not know that you are the temple of God, and that the Spirit of God dwells in you?" (1 Cor 3:16).

Well, do you?

Well then "do you not know that your body is a temple of the Holy Spirit within you?" (1 Cor 6:19).

I think it's important that we allow the Holy Spirit to reveal the truth of these scriptures. You are a temple of God. Oftentimes when we hear this, it is only in reference to taking care of our bodies, and while this is important, I don't think it is the only valuable point. Don't get me wrong, it is vital that we care for our bodies. We need to be good stewards of what God has given us, and caring for this body of ours is one way we can do this. However, it is also true that this body of ours is ultimately passing away. Our being the temple of the Holy Spirit is more than just caring for the temple or the building. Rather, it is grasping the more fundamental reality that the living God dwells in me. That you and I have the holy one dwelling in us. The more we come to understand this the more it changes how we see God and ourselves.

God dwelling in you gives you inestimable value. Think about it, you give singular care and concern for things that have special value. A little boy treats a rookie card of a hall of famer different than that of a player who washed out in the minors. The brand new car is cared for a little differently than that old truck used for hauling junk. Certainly parents expect a young man dating their daughter to treat her with the utmost care given her worth and dignity. And it's the same with each of us. God dwelling in us gives us tremendous worth. Because of this we deserve to be treated with respect and reverence. We deserve to be loved. This doesn't mean we are inappropriately enamored with ourselves, but merely a recognition that God dwells in us and because of this we have value. Therefore it's important that we present ourselves to the world in a manner fitting our worth. We stand before the world confident, we don't need to shrink or cower before the world—nor do we let anyone strip us of our dignity. God himself had made his home with us and we are forever changed.

There is a great firmness in the person who truly grasps that God dwells in him or her. How is it that one can walk through the valley of death and have no fear? This is much easier to comprehend when we are aware that God dwells in us. I don't have to be afraid because God is with me, God lives in me. I need not be concerned about "what may be there" because I know what and who is here. I know who dwells in me. St. John put it this way, "for the one who is in you is greater than the one who is in the world" (1 Jn 4:4). Because of this we can be confident and unafraid.

Finally, if God dwells in me, then I don't need to always go *out there* to find him. So often our search for God has us looking all over. We go to this or that conference, retreat, or holy site looking for God. All of which is fine, but we need to also realize that we don't have to go *out* in order to find God. We ought not forget that God has come to us. When God took flesh in Christ, humanity is forever united to God in a way no one could have imagined. We don't have to go searching for God; he has searched for and found us. And in doing so, God has chosen to send his Spirit to dwell in us. This can change the way we look for God, the way we pray. Probably more often than not, most people pray seeking God outside of themselves. The sense is God is *out there*, and I want God to move from *there* to *here*: my heart, my life, my soul. To be clear, I am not saying that we should not pray that way, but that we don't have to *only* pray that way. We can also pray that we experience his presence in our heart. When we are quiet we can find God who is *inside* us, not only on the outside. Our prayer moves from only looking for and finding God outside to also finding him inside. When we are quiet we look deeply into our hearts, our souls, and we ask God to show himself. When we grow in our ability to discover God who dwells in us, it brings tremendous freedom. The storm may rage around you, but you are at peace because God is in your midst. You will not drown. What happens *out there* is not as much of a concern because the living God is alive in you. You can be confident and unafraid.

Our journey with the Holy Spirit will lead us to many different places. It may be valleys, meadows, mountain tops, and deserts, but wherever he leads be assured that God is present. To the degree that we allow the Spirit to lead us where we need to be, we experience the freedom the Spirit always brings.

Questions for Reflection

1. What would it look like for you to be free? What binds you?

2. What makes you nervous about the Spirit leading you to the desert?

Try This . . .

Ask the Holy Spirit to remind you of a "desert place" in your life. Take a few minutes and remember and feel all that is associated with what the Spirit brings. Finally, ask the Spirit to show you God's presence there.

10

THE SPIRIT LIVES IN THE SACRAMENTS

We need the Holy Spirit in order to be faithful to Jesus. If that's true, and I believe it is, then it is also true that the Church is not able to function without the Holy Spirit. St. Augustine speaks of this dynamic by stating, "What the soul is to man's body, the Holy Spirit is to the Body of Christ, which is the Church."[1] Pope Francis reiterated this by stating, "The Holy Spirit is the soul of the Church."[2]

The Church flows from the Holy Spirit and the Holy Spirit comes from the Church. For this reason, the Church and the Holy Spirit have a beautiful symbiotic relationship. The *Catechism* states that the Church is where we come to know the Holy Spirit. It then goes on to detail several ways this is the case—through the scriptures, tradition, the Magisterium, charisms, prayer, the witness of the saints, and "sacramental liturgy, through its words and symbols, in which the Holy Spirit puts us into communion with Christ" (CCC 688). The sacraments are constitutive of the Church, and it is not possible to have the sacraments apart from the Holy

Spirit. Each and every time we participate in the sacraments of the Church we are encountering the Spirit of God.

What a tremendous gift we have in the sacraments, the channels of grace the Lord has chosen to use for our sanctification and salvation! Every time water is poured, bread is broken, bodies are anointed, or vows are exchanged, the Spirit of God fills those participating with his heavenly grace. I am not sure anyone can fully grasp the power and beauty of the sacraments. Perhaps one of the reasons is that they are so unassuming and humble. Simple elements like water, bread, wine, and oil are used to sustain, heal, and transform us. If it had been up to me (I am glad that it wasn't), perhaps the sacraments could have been designed just a little differently. Imagine if during every sacrament at a specific time, fire, lightning, and thunder miraculously appeared. Now that would get someone's attention. But as we know, God rarely works like that, and he invites us to see the sublime beauty that is present in the symbols of the sacraments. And more importantly, to look through those symbols and see the presence of God.

Sacramental grace starts with Baptism. "Holy Baptism is the basis of the whole Christian life, the gateway to life in the Spirit and the door which gives access to the other sacraments" (CCC 1213). What a great image—the "gateway" to our living a life in the Spirit. In Baptism each of us is brought through this gateway with Christ as the gate (Jn 10:9), and this ushers each of us into a new way of living. We are rescued out of sin that has trapped all humanity, and we are brought into the life of the Trinity. When baptized in the name of the Father, Son, and Holy Spirit we are led into their relationship of unity and love.

Another name for Baptism is "the washing of regeneration and renewal by the Holy Spirit." It signifies and actually brings about the birth of water and the Spirit without which no one "can enter the kingdom of God" (CCC 1215). Baptism begins our relationship with the Holy Spirit.

When we are baptized we become a new creation: pure, holy, and undefiled. We become the very image and likeness of God and the only thing greater than us is God himself. I often think back to watching *Roots* as child. *Roots* was a TV series about the life of Kunte Kinte, an African brought to America as a slave. In one particularly poignant scene, Kunte Kinte wraps his newborn daughter, Kizzy, in a blanket and then takes her outdoors to the top of a hill. It is a starlit night. Kunte unwraps his beautiful daughter from the blanket and holds her up to the heavens and declares, "Kizzy, behold the only thing greater than yourself." It is a very moving scene. With the backdrop of the universe, arrayed with billions of stars and the immensity of God's creation, is a humble, helpless baby who is also the glory of God.

When I baptize infants, if possible, I present to the parents the option of a full immersion Baptism. I think full immersion provides a powerful image, even though it may make the parents a little nervous. I love the look on the parents' faces as they unwrap the baby from the blanket and carefully hand over their precious child to me. I can read the mom's eyes:

"Oh, please Father, don't drop her."

"Relax, I got this."

I then gently take the baby and for a second or two hold her over the Baptismal font. If she is sleeping, that is about to change. Three times she is plunged (the literal meaning of baptize) into the water: Father, Son, Holy Spirit—each time coming out of the water being raised up toward God. I then quickly hand the baby back to Mom before our new Christian has a little accident. The mom, with a look of relief and a warm blanket, welcomes the little one back to her care.

Every time I have participated in a Baptism such as this, the reaction from the congregation has been the same: joy and celebration. On several occasions the faith community has spontaneously begun clapping and cheering. I didn't need to explain to them that what was taking place had eternal significance—they all know it. There are few things comparable to the beauty and dignity of a newly baptized Christian.

But a newly married couple is close. It is such a blessing to be able to witness a young man and woman standing before God, the Church, family, friends—the world—and proclaiming that they desire to love one another as Christ loves the Church. The young couple is inviting the world to witness, in the love they have for each other, the love that Christ has for each of us. What a courageous and bold invitation! One that is impossible to be faithful to without the Holy Spirit. Of course the couple is not left to do this by their own strength: "In this sacrament the spouses receive the Holy Spirit as the communion of love of Christ and the Church. The Holy Spirit is the seal of their covenant, the ever available source of their love and the strength to renew their fidelity" (CCC 1624). The Holy Spirit is "ever available" to the couple, not simply on the wedding day, but all days. As is the case with any vocation, marriage is holy, beautiful, and at times, difficult. It is good for married couples to keep in mind, particularly in difficult times, that the Holy Spirit is "ever available" to strengthen their love and marriage bond.

This was particularly true for some friends of mine. They had been married for about fifteen years with three children. They both said that nothing really bad had happened in their marriage but through a retreat they came to realize that their marriage had largely become "a functional partnership." They each did what needed to be done in order to make it through the day. School pick-up, practice drop-off, grocery shopping, work: it had become the same routine. Each person did their part to make everything work, but at some point (they weren't totally sure when) things seemed to change. Their marriage lacked the life it once had. Even their faith had become routine which had slipped to basically only Mass on Sunday. Their opportunity to get away on retreat brought to light how things had slipped from them. They knew that they needed the Lord's help and his intervention or they feared they would continue to grow apart. After some prayer and discussion they decided that they would go together to an Adoration Chapel twice a month. They began doing this and just spending time before the Lord together. The husband shared with me that it has been a place of great blessing for them. It provides them intentional time with each other and with the Lord. He also shared that after Adoration they will often stop for a coffee and spend more time talking. He was surprised how such a simple thing has had such a great impact both individually and in their marriage.

CONFIRMING THE SPIRIT

The sacrament that most people connect to the Holy Spirit is probably Confirmation. Many people may not know specifically what is taking place at Confirmation, but they know it has something to do with receiving the Holy Spirit. But what exactly does that mean?

First keep in mind that Confirmation is one of the sacraments of initiation (Baptism, Eucharist, and Confirmation) and they should be seen as united. This is somewhat difficult given that in the Roman Rite they are not administered together, but the three really should be seen as a part of a whole: the sacraments of Christian initiation. In Baptism we are freed from sin and brought into a life in the Spirit. When we participate in the Eucharist we are able to receive the body and blood of Christ and are brought into a more complete relationship with Jesus. At Confirmation we receive another outpouring of the Holy Spirit that brings specific gifts to help us live this life in the Spirit. Confirmation is necessary for the completion of the grace of Baptism, and through Confirmation, baptized Christians "are more perfectly bound to the Church and are enriched with a special strength of the Holy Spirit. Hence they are, as true witnesses of Christ, more strictly obliged to spread and defend the faith by word and deed" (CCC 1285).

Acts 8:6–17 is a scripture that the Church looks to regarding Confirmation and a special outpouring of the Spirit. Philip was ministering in Samaria and men and women are coming to faith through his ministry and are being baptized. The apostles in Jerusalem heard of this and sent Peter and John to the new converts. Peter and John, "went down and prayed for them, that they might receive the Holy Spirit, for it had not yet fallen upon any of them; they had only been baptized in the name of the Lord Jesus. Then they laid hands on them and they received the Holy Spirit" (Acts 8:16–17). St. John Paul II commented on this text: "This episode shows us the connection which existed from the Church's earliest days between Baptism and an 'imposition of hands,' a new sacramental act to receive and confer the gift of the Holy Spirit. This rite is considered to be a completion of Baptism." John Paul II goes on to say that the particular grace given in Confirmation is "strength" so that the confirmed is able to be a more effective witness to Christ (General Audience, April, 1992). At Confirmation, when the bishop (or occasionally the priest) lays hands on us he is once again asking for more of the Holy Spirit. Christ knew that we would not be able to live the Christian life on our own power and provides us in Confirmation yet another opportunity to receive the Holy Spirit.

THE HOLY SPIRIT IN THE HOLY EUCHARIST

The last words spoken by Jesus in Matthew's gospel are "behold, I will be with you for all times" (Mt 28:20), and then he leaves, he ascends to heaven.

I wonder what the apostles must have thought. "Hmmm, well, that was odd." I don't think at that moment they fully understood what Jesus meant. "I will be with you always," and then he disappears? How lucky we are to be able to see these events with more understanding than that of the apostles.

"I will be with you always." Jesus fulfills this promise by sending his Holy Spirit and by the gift of the Eucharist. The night before Jesus died he promised that he would not leave the apostles orphans and that he would send another advocate to be with them forever (Jn 14:16–18). Jesus promises that he will be with them, and us, in the person of his Holy Spirit. At that same meal Jesus also assured us that he would be present in his body, the Eucharist. Before his death, Jesus vowed that he would come to us in body and in spirit. Every time we receive Jesus in the Eucharist we receive both his body and spirit. Are we able to see how God is present to us in the Eucharist?

I have often wondered what it would be like if we could see all of the "invisible waves" that are all around us. It would be interesting to have special power that allowed me to see WiFi, infrared, different radio frequencies, wireless waves, electromagnetic waves, microwaves, ocean waves, and so forth. Stuff is all around us, and I just think it would be cool to be able to see it.

I also wonder what it would be like to fully see the many ways that God is present and active in the liturgy. We often go to Mass, and it becomes so ritualistic that I think we miss so much. We just go through the motions and unfortunately fail to see the beauty and mystery that is taking place. St. Bonaventure stated, "The Holy Mass is as full of mysteries as the ocean is as full of drops and the sky is full of stars."[3] How blessed are we?

Fortunately, I don't need special powers to grow in my ability to recognize God's presence. The Holy Spirit is very capable and is eminently willing to help me. If we want this grace to see God's presence, then we actually need to ask for assistance before Mass starts. A simple prayer such as "Come Holy Spirit, let me see and experience Christ in this holy Mass" is sure to yield fruit. Ask the Holy Spirit to open the eyes of your heart so that you are able to see God's presence in the people who are gathering for Mass. So often we walk by people and don't greet them or have any real interest in knowing their story. God is present in each person; pray that you are able to recognize him.

Also ask the Holy Spirit to bring alive in your heart the scriptures as they are proclaimed. Recall that the Holy Spirit is present in the Word of God and the Spirit brings the Word alive. The liturgy is such a wonderful place to experience this.

At the beginning of the consecration the priest, acting in the person of Christ, prays that the Father would send his Spirit upon the bread and wine in order that they may become Jesus' body and blood. This prayer is called the *epiclesis* which literally means "calling down the Holy Spirit." The priest holds his hands over the bread and wine and prays, and depending on which Eucharistic prayer he chooses, you may hear:

> Make Holy, therefore we pray by sending down your Spirit upon them like the dewfall, so that they may become for us the body and blood of our Lord Jesus Christ (Eucharistic Prayer 2).

> By the power and working of the Holy Spirit you give life to all things . . . by that same Spirit graciously make

holy these gifts we have brought to you for consecration (Eucharistic Prayer 3).

The same Spirit that was present to Jesus at the Last Supper the night before he died is once again present to us in the eternal offering of the Mass. The Spirit that blessed Jesus as he prayed with and taught his disciples at that holy meal blesses and changes humble bread into the body of Jesus. The *Catechism* teaches:

> At the heart of the Eucharistic celebration are the bread and wine that, by the words of Christ and the invocation of the Holy Spirit, become Christ's Body and Blood. Faithful to the Lord's command the Church continues to do, in his memory and until his glorious return, what he did on the eve of his Passion: "He took bread. . . . He took the cup filled with wine" (1333).

I am so blessed that I am able to participate in the Mass every day. I don't know exactly what next Thursday is going to look like, or what I will be doing June 7, 2028, but what I do know is that if God allows it, I will be participating in the Eucharist on those days. In the Eucharist, I am able to encounter Jesus and can't imagine not taking the opportunity for such a graced appointment.

The Holy Spirit helps to facilitate this encounter. Coming to believe that Jesus is truly present in the Eucharist is a gift of the Spirit. When the disciples stated how hard it was to accept Jesus' teaching about his flesh being real food, Jesus responded, "Does this shock you? What if you were to see the Son of Man ascending to where he was before? It is the *spirit* that gives life, while the flesh is of no avail. The words I have spoken to you are spirit and life" (Jn 6:61–63). St. John Paul II, reflecting on this, stated, "The Master immediately explained that his words would be clarified and understood only through the 'Spirit, the giver of life.'" John Paul II goes on to point out that immediately after Pentecost the early followers of Jesus "devoted themselves to the breaking of bread and prayers" (Acts 2:42). From the beginning of the Church's history the breaking of the bread was key to our life together. He concluded his reflection on the Eucharist and the Holy Spirit by adding: "At the center of the Church is the Eucharist, where Christ is present and active in humanity and in the whole world by means of the Holy Spirit" (John Paul II, General Audience, September, 1989).

I don't remember a time in my life when I really complained about going to Mass, though it's possible my parents would beg to differ. However, after I experienced more powerfully the Holy Spirit, the Mass took on even more meaning and greater importance. It's as if it all made more sense to me. The Eucharist became more personal. I came to understand that the celebration of the Eucharist was something to which I was personally invited; it mattered that I was there. I began to understand that my participation in the Mass would have an impact on the rest of my week. It wasn't something that I simply just went to, got my card punched and went on with the rest of the week. Rather, the Mass, the grace of the Mass, would sustain me. My being more patient or generous is possible because of the Eucharist.

I also came to understand that it mattered how I approached the Eucharist. I began to go to the Eucharist with a greater sense of purpose and not merely out of obligation. I wanted to be more worthy to come to the altar. I was aware that I would never be fully worthy to receive such a gift, but I wanted to be the best I could. There became a cyclical relationship. When I went to Mass, I encountered God and his Spirit. This encounter provided me grace to be a more faithful witness to the Lord and his goodness. The Spirit of God became more a part of my daily life. As this happened, I had a greater desire to pray as well as to attend Mass.

Then, when I attended Mass I once again encountered God. And so goes the cycle of the Eucharist, the Spirit of God and our life.

I suppose there is a tendency to take for granted those things which are most dear to us. We probably don't tell those we love that we love them as often as we should. How often do we thank the Lord for the sacraments? So many of my greatest memories are associated with the sacraments. While I don't remember my Baptism, I've heard it was fantastic. I do remember my first Communion and the great celebration that it was. Over the years there have been so many confessions that have been pivotal in my walk with the Lord. I know that there is always a place I can go and encounter Jesus and be reminded that my sins are forgiven. My ordination to the priesthood continues to be a source of grace for me and hopefully others as well. The sacraments are such a blessing in my life, and in the lives of all Catholics. I can't imagine my life without the sacraments.

From the time I was an infant the sacraments have been a constant, faithful companion. Any time I may have wondered I always knew that I could return to the sacraments and there I would find grace and familiarity that would comfort and encourage me. The sacraments have aided in my continual conversion and I am so blessed that the Holy Spirit continues to nudge me to them. I pray that the Holy Spirit would continue to place on my heart and yours an even deeper love for and gratitude for the sacraments.

Questions for Reflection

1. What could you do differently to be more prepared to encounter Jesus in the Mass?

2. For those who are married, how could the Holy Spirit be more a part of your marriage?

Try This . . .

"Holy Spirit, show me my sins so that I may know your Mercy."
Wait for it. Now, go to confession within one week and encounter Jesus there.

11
THE SPIRIT GIVES WITNESS

"Does anyone want to give witness?"

I wasn't accustomed to hearing this question asked in any church service and particularly not at a funeral. A friend's son had passed away, and I was blessed by being able to attend the funeral. He wasn't Catholic and was buried from a non-denominational evangelical church. After some lively worship and an extended message from the minister, the floor was opened for anyone to say something.

"Does anyone want to witness?"

Apparently so.

For the next thirty minutes church members took turns standing up and giving witness to God's love and faithfulness. There was an occasional word about the deceased but almost always in connection to God's mercy. This was a beautiful expression of the faith of the people. It was powerful listening to those attending a funeral give witness to Christ and his saving presence.

"Does anyone want to give witness?" I briefly considered ending my next homily with the very same question. Very briefly.

However, when I was the director of the seminary formation for my Franciscan community one of the traditions I started
was what I called "Witness Wednesday" or "Testimony Tuesday"
depending on the semester and the course schedule of the friars.
For the last ten minutes of our dinner the friars were invited to
offer witness to how they had seen God work or how they were
blessed by God during the previous week. You see, it's important
for us as Christians to be able to give witness to God's glory, and it's
also a blessing to hear others give witness. Left to our own devices,
we would rarely do such things, however, the Spirit of God is all
about giving witness.

THE WORD OF GOD

In John 15:26 Jesus says that the Holy Spirit will give witness to
him. How is it that the Spirit gives witness to Jesus? Well, there are
many ways. Jesus states in John that he is "the way, the truth and
the life" (Jn 14:6). In a world and culture that largely denies objec-
tive truth, it is important for Christians to keep in mind that there
is truth and it can be known. Truth is not relative and individuals
are not the source of what is true. The *Catechism* affirms this: "In
Jesus Christ, the whole of God's truth has been made manifest.
"Full of grace and truth," he came as the 'light of the world,' he
is the Truth" (CCC 2466). St. John goes on to assert; "But when
he comes, the Spirit of truth, he will guide you to all truth" (Jn
16:13). The Holy Spirit is always going to lead us to what is true.
It may be at times difficult for us to perceive the truth, but if we
are honest, and are genuinely seeking what is true, the Spirit will
lead us to truth. And what is actually true is often in direct conflict
with what the culture spouts as true. It takes great courage, which
the Spirit also provides (2 Tm 1:7) to be able to say that the world
is wrong. We can stand confident in this. "The Holy Spirit will lead
us into all truth and will glorify Christ. He will prove the world

wrong about sin, righteousness, and judgment" (CCC 729). The Spirit will lead us to the truth, and the truth will set us free.

The Spirit also gives witness through the Word of God, the scriptures. The Church has consistently taught that God is the author of the scriptures and that God blessed men with the Holy Spirit to write down "whatever God wanted written and no more" (CCC 104–105). Obviously, this makes the scriptures different than any other book written and as such it can't be approached merely as a great book written two thousand years ago. It is not just a book with lots of life stories and moral teachings. As the living Word of God, the scriptures are not simply "dead letters." We are invited to pray that Christ, the eternal Word of the living God, must, through the Holy Spirit, "open [our] minds to understand the scriptures" (CCC 108). Without the Holy Spirit the scriptures are merely words on a page. It's impossible to separate the words of the scriptures from the Holy Spirit, hence the Spirit of God desires to bring the words of scripture alive. Reading the scriptures can have a powerful impact in our lives. One example of this is a line in John's gospel. It is John 15:16. "It was not you who chose me, but I who chose you and appointed you to go and bear fruit." I'm not sure when I first read that, but I will never forget reading it as a college student and sensing that God was choosing me to be a priest, and as a priest, my life must bear fruit. Those words stirred in my heart as a twenty-one-year-old undergrad and continue to do so. Only the Spirit can cause that.

The author of Hebrews states as much; "the word of God is living and effective, sharper than any two-edged sword, penetrating even between soul and spirit, joints, and marrow" (Heb 4:12).

The words are no longer just ink on paper but they are spirit and life. The Holy Spirit's witness reveals Jesus as the Christ. The Holy Spirit gives witness to the glory of God that we are not able to come to on our own.

It is the Spirit's witness to Jesus that has inspired and changed the lives of countless men and women. I recall listening to a talk from a man who was in New York City on a business trip. Late one evening he opened the drawer next to his bed and found a bible there. Having been raised without faith, he had never read any of the New Testament. He spent the rest of the evening reading the Gospel of Matthew and the words on the page came alive in his heart, and since then, his life has never been the same. The Holy Spirit witnessed to his soul the truth and power of what he read in the scriptures that eventually moved this man to seek Baptism. There is an important distinction here; it is not as if the words of the scriptures came alive as he read them. The scriptures were already alive. The Spirit does not randomly anoint the words so that they are alive one day and not alive the next. Rather, the Word of God is living and true at all times. What the Spirit does is give witness to that reality in our heart. The Spirit moves on *us* and brings the living Word of God alive in our heart.

The Spirit desires to witness to us as we read the Word of God. I wish I could say that every day when I sit down to read scripture that it is a life-changing experience, but it isn't like that. At times I read them and it just feels like I am going through the motions. It seems like they don't have anything to say to me. Other times, what I read changes how I see God and myself.

I recall one time when I was on retreat in Arizona. I was reading the text in Romans where St. Paul says that God is on our side (Rom 8:31). Now, I know I had read that scripture several times before; it was highlighted in yellow so clearly it was not new to me. But there was something different this time. When reading it this time, I had the profound insight that God really is for me, he is on my side. I think sometimes if we are honest we think God is "on the other side" or that he is against us. Kind of like he is a police officer. I know that the police are tasked to "protect and serve," but a small part of me feels that their real job is to "catch us" if we do something wrong. Oftentimes we can be tempted to think that God is in the heavens and is really just watching, waiting for us to mess up so that he can punish us or be disappointed in us. That simply is not true. God is for us, he is on our side, and God is rooting for us; he is encouraging us. At that moment in Arizona, I came alive and understood this to be true.

On that particular day, reading that God was for me, something was different. I had such a deep awareness that God was close and, at that moment, any sense of an adversarial God was gone. As I read that scripture the Spirit gave witness to me, illuminated the text so that I could see God differently. It was another moment of conversion for me. I knew more personally that God was for me and I was able to approach God with more confidence, and honestly, more love.

OUR WORDS

In a really wonderful scene in Acts, Peter is called in front of the council leaders to be chastised for speaking about Jesus (Acts 5:27–32). Recall that this is the same Peter who was previously hiding in a room out of fear. Now he is being dragged before the authorities. Peter is reminded that he was not to speak about Jesus or the resurrection. My suspicion is that Peter didn't really forget that he wasn't supposed to talk about Jesus; rather, he didn't care what they said he could or could not speak about. Peter proclaims that he *must* obey God and give witness to Jesus. He points out that the Spirit gives witness and so must he. The Spirit uses Peter, his words and actions, to give witness to Jesus, and this infuriates the leaders who want to put Peter to death.

For the early Church to grow and develop, it was imperative that the apostles and other followers of Jesus give witness to what had happened. They needed to tell what they had seen and experienced. The Holy Spirit blessed the works and words of the apostles as they gave witness to Jesus. The apostles spoke, the Holy Spirit anointed their words, and this moved the hearts of all who listened.

I like the story of the conversion of the Ethiopian in Acts 8. While Philip is traveling on a road heading south from Jerusalem, the Holy Spirit instructs him to approach a chariot and basically hitch a ride. When Philip does this he meets an Ethiopian official who was reading the scripture but didn't understand what he was reading. The official asks if Philip might be able to help him. "Then Philip opened his mouth and, beginning with this scripture passage, he proclaimed Jesus to him" (Acts 8:35). The official came to faith through the words of Philip and was baptized.

Only the Holy Spirit can take ordinary words, sounds from one's mouth, and bless them so that they have the power to change another person's heart. These words can bring healing, hope, and freedom.

This is what happened with the apostles' words.

The Spirit gave power to their words and brought their words to life.

This continues to happen today. The Spirit uses ordinary people's words to give witness to Jesus and to change lives. So many times I have heard people speak about Jesus and their words penetrate my heart. In a moment their words cut to my soul and I am able to see Jesus more clearly. Sometimes the word leads me to repentance while other times I am filled with joy. This only happens when the Spirit gives witness to the realities of God.

I have been on the other side of this as well. I have had individuals approach me and say to me, "I attended a conference you spoke at eight years ago. What you said that day changed my life." I find encounters such as this both moving and humbling. Words that come out of my mouth have the power to change a person's life! To be clear, I don't believe that my words alone can change anyone's life. I do, however, believe that when I speak the Holy Spirit can bless my words and give witness to Jesus through them. God is the one who does amazing things. This is why I always ask the Holy Spirit to fill me and bless me as I prepare a homily or talk. As I work, I continually ask for the Holy Spirit's guidance. I first pray that the scriptures would come alive in *my* heart as I read and pray over them. I pray that the Spirit would give witness to the words I am reading and that I would experience the grace of God. I ask that I will be more converted through my study of the Word of God.

I also ask the Spirit to bring to my mind pertinent stories and examples that will connect with the people who will be present when I preach. Finally, I pray for the Spirit's help with the delivery of the talk or homily. It may sound trite, but it's true—a priest's words have the potential to save someone's life. We as priests need to continually take seriously the sacred trust Christ has given us as we preach. Our preaching will be most effective when we are preaching in the Spirit rather than merely sharing our own thoughts or words.

Here's something that is also important: those who listen to homilies also need to pray. (Praying that the homily end quickly is not what I mean.) The responsibility for the homily to touch the heart of the listener is not to be borne only by the priest. When was the last time you prayed before a homily that God would open your heart? Even a simple prayer such as: "God please bless Father as he preaches this morning. May the Holy Spirit bless his words that they may stir in my heart. Open my heart and mind so that I may receive all you have for me. Holy Spirit give witness to Jesus by his words." It doesn't matter how good the preacher is or how powerful the words being spoken, if there is not fertile soil in the soul to receive that word, it will not grow. The person preaching may give a wonderful homily, but the seed may fall on poor soil. And the opposite may also be true. Someone might give a poor homily, but the Spirit can move in what is said and heard to bring about tremendous blessing. It's a powerful experience when both the preacher and the listener are seeking the Holy Spirit. Take a minute or two before Mass and ask God to open your heart that the Spirit may give witness.

WITNESS AND EVANGELIZATION

By now I suspect, hope, pray, wonder if every Catholic knows that evangelization, witnessing to their faith, is every Christian's responsibility. Pope Benedict XVI stated in *Verbum Domini* that "the mission of proclaiming the word of God is the task of all the disciples of Jesus Christ based on their Baptism" (Article 94). Every Catholic has the invitation and task to share their faith, to witness to the glory of God. While every Catholic has *the task*, many freak out at the thought of actually evangelizing. I think there are two main reasons why so many Catholics have this reaction toward evangelization: fear and lack of knowledge. Or is it lack of knowledge and fear? I struggle with which to list first.

I think Catholics struggle because lately they are hearing more about their need to evangelize, but often don't know what that really means for them. They are being asked to do something but are not clear on what it is they are being asked to do.

The fact remains that many Catholics are being asked to evangelize but don't really know what that means or how to do it. A sure-fire way to frustrate someone is to expect them to do something that they don't know how to do. I remember when I was young and in school the teacher asking me to do a math problem that I didn't know how to do. Of course, I found myself frustrated. If I am taught how to do the math problem, I am not going to stress the next time I am asked.

So it is with evangelization. We need to learn how to evangelize and what is meant by evangelization.

Then, we need to get past fear. Now, one of the reasons so many people are fearful is because they don't know what they are doing. But once that is taken care of, there still remains fear about actually witnessing to their faith. Thank God that these are not insurmountable obstacles—the more we do something the less frightening it becomes.

Finally, and this is key and should come as no surprise, it is the Holy Spirit who is ultimately the evangelizer. Pope Paul VI wrote in *Evangelization in the Modern World*, "Evangelization is never possible without the Holy Spirit. . . . It must be said that the Holy Spirit is the principal agent of evangelization: it is he who impels each individual to proclaim the Gospel, and it is he who in the depths of consciences causes the word of salvation to be accepted and understood" (Article 76). The Holy Spirit moves in me to reach out in some way in order to share the Gospel and at the same time moves in the heart of the person to whom I am reaching out. This should come as a great relief. Evangelization is not totally dependent on you or your giftedness; it is simply our response to the movement of the Spirit. What could be easier than that?

If the Holy Spirit is the evangelizer, then this must mean we can just get out of the way and let the Spirit do the Spirit's thing, right? Well, kind of, but not totally. Yes, we need to get out of the Spirit's way, but we also need to cooperate with the Spirit in order to further the kingdom of God. We effectively do this through a few simple things.

First what is meant by evangelization? Very simply, it is bringing the Good News, the light of Jesus Christ, into every human situation. It is proclaiming that while we were sinners, Christ loved us and gave his life for us (Rom 5:8), and if we repent of our sins and believe in Jesus, we can inherit eternal life (Jn 3:16).

Pope Francis has encouraged us to get back to the basics of our faith. It's very helpful if we understand what the basic tenets of our faith are. St. John Paul II, Pope Benedict XVI, and Pope Francis have all encouraged the Church to return to a basic *keryg-matic* message. The *kerygma* is a Greek word that literally means "to preach," but used in this context it is the basics of our faith. There are basically four points and it's helpful for all Catholics to know these:

1. God loves us.
2. We have each sinned and walked away from God's love.
3. Jesus came to earth and suffered, died, and rose from the dead to save us.
4. We each need to accept this and live our life for Christ in relationship with the Body of Christ, the Church.

In order for us to be more effective witnesses, this basic message needs to be a part of our story. I am able to speak about each of these four points. I can talk about experiences of God's love and am able to share that story. I am able to share how I have sinned but more importantly about how I experienced God's mercy. Finally, I can speak about the many times I have chosen to live my life for Christ and how he continues to rescue me.

My story is my story and you have yours. Don't forget that your story is extremely important. How have you experienced God's love? When did you encounter Jesus? Sure, Jesus came to rescue humanity, but how did he rescue you? What is your story? What has your life been like since you decided to follow Jesus? Be honest. For ninety-nine percent of people, following Christ is not just bubbles and rainbows—there are times when it is diffi-cult. Freely discussing our struggles helps us connect with other people's experiences in life. Admitting difficulty makes us more credible, not less.

If you are able to allow the Holy Spirit to make these four simple points a part of your story, you are well on your way to being a more effective witness for Christ.

This leads to another point: being a witness to Jesus is not simply a singular event at a particular place and time. Singular events are important—they can be graced moments when we are with someone and are being invited to share something of our faith. When the Spirit is stirring in our heart to say (email, mail, text, or call someone) or do something, it is important that we respond to this. Those moments can be very powerful experiences for us as well as the person with whom we are sharing.

But we need also to see our *life* as a witness to God. It's essential to move from an attitude of thinking that giving witness to God is an occasional activity to realizing that our giving witness is a way of life. My prayer is that my life would give witness to Jesus. It is by living our life in relationship with the Holy Spirit that we move from only singular moments of witness to a life of witness. If we are in continual relationship with the Spirit of God and not only checking in occasionally, then our lives are able to be a more consistent witness to Jesus.

The opportunities for us to be able to witness to God's goodness are literally endless. As Christians our lives are supposed to witness to the world about the God we worship. How we forgive teaches the world how Christ forgives. How we love shows God's love. What kind of lesson are we giving? Like it or not, aware of it or not, our lives bear witness to something. Let us pray that our lives would be light in a world that so desperately longs to see.

Questions for Reflection

1. How have you seen God work in your life this week? Be specific.

2. There are people who may never experience Christ unless you share him with them. Thoughts?

Try This . . .

Ask the Holy Spirit to help you give witness to God's goodness. Take a blank piece of paper and note the four elements of the *kerygma* listed on page 134. With each point jot down your personal story and how it relates to each element. How have you experienced God's love? What is a time when you came to understand that you have sinned, you have failed, and that you need God? How did Jesus make himself personal to you? When did you decide to follow God and how has your life changed since you made the decision? Within one week share this with someone. Not sure who to talk to? Ask the Holy Spirit.

12
THE SPIRIT HELPS US TO REMEMBER

I'm pretty good at remembering things. I hardly ever forget something when I travel, though there was that one time when I went to the Holy Land and left my Franciscan habit hanging on the back of my door at the friary. Thank the Lord one of the people I worked with was coming after me and was able to pick it up. But by and large, I don't forget a lot of stuff and the reason I don't is I try to make sure I have reminders.

I set myself multiple alarms for things that I need to remember. Sometimes my life gets a little hectic and it helps to have reminders. I love the fact that my computer and my phone talk with each other and remind each other to remind me about events and commitments I have made.

There are, however, things I don't remember. You see, I have the type of mind that doesn't remember a lot of facts. If I have written it down or can look it up somewhere, I often don't remember. Like saints' feast days. Some people know the feast day of every saint; I don't have a clue about ninety-nine percent of them. Sure, I remember my biggies—St. Francis, St. Anthony, St. Paul,

and, well I'm sure I know more. I just don't have a memory for
certain things and at times this surprises people. More than once
I have heard, "Oh, I thought you would know that since you are
a priest."

OK. On one hand, priests don't know *everything* about *every*
church-related topic, and on the other hand, I know even less. Take,
for instance, the gospel writers. I know that there are four. I know
their names: Matthew, Mark, Luke, and John. So far so good. But
I can never remember the symbols that represent them nor where
in Revelation they are referenced. I can remember that John is the
eagle because his theology kind of soars like an eagle. But the other
three, I *always* forget. (Matthew is a winged man-angel, Mark is
a lion, and Luke is an ox, and it is referenced in Revelation 4:7. I
looked it up.) I know, I know, I've heard it a million times. "I would
think a priest would remember that." Well, this one doesn't. I just
don't remember things that I can easily find the answer should I
need to.

And perhaps the disciples also had difficulty remembering
things. This may be why Jesus said to them, "The Advocate, the
holy Spirit that the Father will send in my name—he will teach
you everything and remind you of all that I told you" (Jn 14:26).

It's easy for us to forget. A friend of mine once said that we
won't forget things that are important to us; I don't know that I
agree. On more occasions than I care to remember God has needed
to remind me of his love for me. Often times I have found myself
sitting in my chapel alone and frustrated, wondering why God
isn't doing my will. When I have wallowed just the right amount
of time, the Spirit reminds me that I am loved. I usually go on to
explain that this is not the issue and proceed to explain to God
what the real issue is. God listens patiently and reminds me that I
am loved. Do I know that God loves me? Yes, of course. Do I need
to be reminded? Even more.

I often joke that ninety-five percent of my ministry is reminding people of things that they know or have already heard. In some ways that is kind of frustrating; I mean, I would love to say something so totally original that everyone proclaims, "That's amazing, I have never heard such a thing." But more often than not what I get is, "That's it, God loves me?" Yep, pretty much. But to that end, I think it is cooperating with the Spirit to be able to remind each other the truths of our faith.

Memory is key in the spiritual life. When Jesus said, "do this in remembrance of me" (Luke 22:19; 1 Corinthians 11:24), I don't think it was just a suggestion. Jesus wants us to remember. Obviously, this is central to the Eucharist, which is, by its nature, a remembering. The Mass is not only a mental remembering but a remembering that makes present Christ's saving actions. It's not being able to remember so that you are able to pass an exam at the end of your life. Rather, it is remembering so that your life can be more filled with God's blessing, his presence, and his life. The more you are able to remember who God is and what he has done for you the greater peace you will experience.

It's important for us to remember this: the Holy Spirit is present to us in order to fill our life with God. The Spirit brings love, peace, and joy, but first and foremost, the Spirit brings God. The Holy Spirit doesn't only work in the past but is working today. Not only does the Spirit work in the lives of the saints but also in the lives of sinners like you and me. The truly miraculous thing is that the very same Spirit is making us—who are weak—into saints who are strong. My prayer is not that this transformation takes place someday in the future. Rather, I pray that the Spirit of God come to us today, this very moment, and continue his transforming work in our lives. In order for this to happen, we need God's Spirit to remind us all that Jesus has revealed. I continually pray that God's Spirit will always help us remember:

- God is love (1 Jn 4:8).
- God sent his only Son so that whoever believes in him may have eternal life (Jn 3:16).
- The Spirit enables us to proclaim Jesus as Lord (Rom 12:3).
- The Spirit gives witness to the Resurrection of Jesus (Acts 4:33).
- The Spirit has been poured into our hearts (Rom 5:5).
- The Spirit makes us holy (1 Pt 1:2).
- The Spirit empowers us (Acts 1:8).
- The Spirit breathes on us (Jn 20:22).
- The Spirit brings peace (Rom 14:17).
- The Spirit brings joy (1 Thes 1:6).
- The Spirit teaches us to pray (Rom 8:26–27).
- The Spirit fills us (Eph 5:18).
- The Spirit convicts us of our sin (Jn 16:8).
- The Spirit brings freedom (2 Cor 3:17).
- We have not received a spirit of slavery, but a spirit of adoption that cries out *Abba*, Father (Rom 8:16).
- The Spirit generously gives gifts of wisdom, understanding, counsel, fortitude, knowledge, fear of the Lord, and piety (Is 11:2–3; CCC 1831).
- The Spirit produces fruit in our life: love, joy, peace, patience, kindness, generosity, faithfulness, gentleness, and self-control (Gal 5:22–23).
- The Spirit comforts us (Acts 9:31).
- The Spirit gives spiritual gifts (1 Cor 12).
- The Spirit helps us to reap eternal life (Gal 6:8).
- The Spirit gives us access to God the Father (Eph 2:18).
- The Spirit casts out demons (Mt 12:28).

- The Spirit changes bread and wine into Christ's body and blood (Jn 6:54; CCC 1333).
- The Spirit reveals truth (Jn 16:13).
- The Spirit helps us remember (Jn 14:26).

The Holy Spirit is our comforter, our shield, and protector. My prayer is that we all come to know that beauty, freedom, joy, and love that comes in surrendering our life to the Spirit of God. I pray that you constantly seek to live your life in relationship with God's Spirit who is the Lord and giver of life.

Finally, I pray that the Holy Spirit, the Wild Goose, may share his "wildness" with you and you come to know and experience the glory that is living your life totally and radically surrendered to the Spirit of God.

> Come Holy Spirit, fill the hearts of your faithful
> And kindle in them the fire of your love.
> Send forth your Spirit and they shall be created.
> And you shall renew the face of the earth.
> O, God, who by the light of the Holy Spirit,
> Did instruct the hearts of the faithful,
> Grant that by the same Holy Spirit we may be truly wise
> And ever rejoice in His consolations,
> Through Christ Our Lord, Amen.

NOTES

INTRODUCTION

1. "Apostolic Journey to Turkey: Holy Mass at the Catholic Cathedral of the Holy Spirit," *news.va*, November 29, 2014, accessed February 23, 2015, www.news.va/en/news/apostolic-journey-to-turkey-holy-mass-at-the-catho.

2. THE SPIRIT IS GENEROUS TO US

1. Fr. Bernhard Blankenhorn, "The Seven Gifts of the Holy Spirit Sunday Adult Education Forum @ Blessed Sacrament Parish March 18, 2007," *blessed-sacrament.org*, March 18, 2007, accessed February 23, 2015, www.blessed-sacrament.org/sevengifts.doc.

2. "Gift of Wisdom: Pope Francis Begins Series of Talks on the Gifts of the Holy Spirit," *catholiconline.org*, April 12, 2014, accessed February 23, 2015, www.catholic.org/news/international/europe/story.php?id=54889.

3. Ibid.

4. "Pope Francis Teaches On the Spiritual Gift of Understanding," *catholiconline.org*, May 1, 2014, accessed February 23, 2015, www.catholic.org/news/international/europe/story.php?id=55220.

5. "Pope Francis: The Gift of Counsel Illuminates the Heart," *ncregister.com*, May 7, 2014, accessed February 23, 2015, www.ncregister.com/daily-news/pope-francis-the-gift-of-counsel-illuminates-the-heart/.

6. "Audience: The Gift of Fortitude," *en.radiovaticana.va*, May, 14, 2014, accessed February 23, 2015, en.radiovaticana.va/storico/2014/05/14/audience_the_gift_of_fortitude/en1-799087.

7. "Gift of Knowledge Attunes Us to Vision of God, Pope Says," *catholicnewsagency.com*, May 21, 2014, accessed February 23, 2015, www.catholicnewsagency.com/news/gift-of-knowledge-attunes-us-to-vision-of-god-pope-says.

8. "Pope Francis on the Gift of Piety," *news.va*, June 4, 2014, accessed February 23, 2015, www.news.va/en/news/pope-francis-on-the-gift-of-piety.

9. Pope Francis, "General Audience: St. Peter's Square Wednesday, 11 June 2014," *w2.vatican.va*, June 11, 2014, accessed February 23, 2015, w2.vatican.va/content/francesco/en/audiences/2014/documents/papa-francesco_20140611_udienza-generale.html.

3. THE SPIRIT GIVES US GIFTS

1. "Pope Francis Discovers Charismatic Movement a Gift to the Whole Church," *catholicnews.com*, August 9, 2013, accessed February 23, 2015, www.catholicnews.com/data/stories/cns/1303443.htm.

2. "Pope Francis Celebrates Charismatic Movement at Rome's Olympic Stadium," *zenit.org*, June 2, 2014, accessed February 23, 2015, www.zenit.org/en/articles/francis-celebrates-charismatic-movement-at-rome-s-olympic-stadium.

3. "Apostolic Journey to Turkey: Holy Mass at the Catholic Cathedral of the Holy Spirit," *news.va*, November 29, 2014, accessed February 23, 2015, www.news.va/en/news/apostolic-journey-to-turkey-holy-mass-at-the-catho.

5. THE SPIRIT BAPTIZES US

1. Francis A. Sullivan, *Charisms and Charismatic Renewal: A Biblical and Theological Study* (Eugene, OR: Wipf and Stock Publishers, 2004), 70–72.

2. "Do Not Cage the Holy Spirit, Pope Tells Massive Rome Gathering," *catholicnewsagency.com*, June 2, 2014, accessed February 23, 2015, http://www.catholicnewsagency.com/news/do-not-cage-the-holy-spirit-pope-tells-massive-rome-gathering.

3. "Pope's Homily at Mass on the Feast of the Baptism of the Lord," *zenit.org*, January 11, 2015, accessed February 23, 2015, www.zenit.org/en/articles/pope-s-homily-at-mass-on-the-feast-of-the-baptism-of-the-lord.

6. THE SPIRIT IS UNLIMITED TO US

1. "Pope at Mass: A Healthy Christian is a Joyful Christian," *news.va*, May 23, 2014, accessed February 23, 2015, www.news.va/en/news/pope-at-mass-a-healthy-christian-is-a-joyful-chris.

7. THE SPIRIT ADOPTS US

1. "Pope: Only Holy Spirit Can Speak to Our Hearts of God's Love," *zenit.org*, May 9, 2013, accessed February 23, 2015, http://www.zenit.org/en/articles/pope-only-holy-spirit-can-speak-to-our-hearts-of-god-s-love.

10. THE SPIRIT LIVES IN THE SACRAMENTS

1. Rev. Peter Stravinskas, "The Holy Spirit in the Sacraments," *catholiceducation.org*, accessed February 23, 2015, www.catholiceducation.org/en/culture/catholic-contributions/the-holy-spirit-in-the-sacraments.html.

2. "Apostolic Journey to Turkey: Holy Mass at the Catholic Cathedral of the Holy Spirit," *news.va*, November 29, 2014, accessed February 23, 2015, www.news.va/en/news/apostolic-journey-to-turkey-holy-mass-at-the-catho.

3. Fr. Barry O'Sullivan, "Reflections on the Celebration of Mass," *holyspiritinteractive.net*, accessed February 23, 2015, www.holyspiritinteractive.net/columns/guests/barryosullivan/themass.asp.

Rev. Dave Pivonka, T.O.R., is the director of Franciscan Pathways and has served for more than thirty years as a spiritual director, retreat leader, and formation director. He is a well-known conference speaker and pilgrimage leader. Fr. Pivonka is active in charismatic renewal and serves on the board of Renewal Ministries. Fr. Pivonka is the author of several books, including *Spiritual Freedom* and *Hiking the Camino*. He lives in Pittsburgh, Pennsylvania.